GLOBETROTTER™

Travel Guide

BERMUDA

ROBIN AND JENNY McKELVIE

NH
NEW HOLLAND

NEW
HOLLAND

★★★ Highly recommended
★★ Recommended
★ See if you can

First edition published in 2007
by New Holland Publishers (UK) Ltd
London • Cape Town • Sydney • Auckland
First published in 1994
10 9 8 7 6 5 4 3 2 1

website: www.newhollandpublishers.com

Garfield House, 86 Edgware Road
London W2 2EA, United Kingdom

80 McKenzie Street
Cape Town 8001, South Africa

14 Aquatic Drive, Frenchs Forest
NSW 2086, Australia

218 Lake Road, Northcote
Auckland, New Zealand

Distributed in the USA by
The Globe Pequot Press, Connecticut

ISBN 978 1 84 537 451 8

Keep us Current
Information in travel guides is apt to change, which
is why we regularly update our guides. We'd be
grateful to receive feedback if you've noted something we should include in our updates. If you have
new information, please share it with us by writing to
the Publishing Manager, Globetrotter, at the office
nearest to you (addresses on this page). The most
significant contribution to each new edition will
receive a free copy of the updated guide.

Although every effort has been made to ensure that
this guide is up to date and current at time of going
to print, the Publisher accepts no responsibility or
liability for any loss, injury or inconvenience
incurred by readers or travellers using this guide.

Publishing Manager: Thea Grobbelaar
DTP Cartographic Manager: Genené Hart
Editor: Alicha van Reenen
Picture Researcher: Shavonne Govender
Designer: Nicole Bannister
Cartographer: Nicole Bannister

Reproduction by Resolution, Cape Town.
Printed and bound by Times Offset (M) Sdn. Bhd.,
Malaysia.

Photographic credits:
All photographs by **Robin McKelvie**, except the
following:
page 22: **Doug Pearson/jonarnoldimages.com**
pages 21 and 35: **Peter Baker/International
PhotoBank**.

Cover: *Pastel coloured buildings peering out
over the harbour from Hamilton City's bustling
Front Street.*
Title page: *A ferry transporting passengers from the
waterfront at Hamilton City.*

CONTENTS

1
Introducing
Bermuda

*C*ould you but view the scenery fair, That now *beneath my window lies, You'd think that Nature lavished there, Her purest wave, her softest skies*. The Irish poet Tom Moore is but one of a long list of artistic luminaries and famous figures, such as Mark Twain, the British royal family and Michael Douglas, who have been charmed by Bermuda's beauty and have waxed lyrical on these special, subtropical islands. The hype for once is more than justified by a necklace of around 181 (only a sprinkling of which are inhabited) islands that lie improbably adrift in the deep Atlantic, awash with pink sand beaches and lush vegetation, encircled by a dazzling coral reef.

You have to admire an oasis whose motto is *Quo Fata Ferunt*, or 'Where the Fates take us', perhaps due to the fact that Bermuda was settled not by design, but by accident when a hurricane hurled ashore a British ship. Forced to spend time on the islands to build replacement boats, the new arrivals soon fell in love with the virgin territory and man has remained similarly enamoured ever since, with tourism now a major industry, whether it be those spending a week or more in the grand resort hotels or just passing by for a day or two on one of the ubiquitous summer cruise ships.

Bermuda is genuinely unique in the modern world. With a population of only 64,000, commuters are welcomed to the capital each morning by a man waving and wishing everyone a good day, the speed limit is a soporific 35kph (22mph) and a cricket match is an integral part of a two-day holiday. This may not be the

Opposite: *Sunrise over the sands of Elbow Beach.*

Above: *Typical business attire: Bermuda shorts, hose and blazer.*

FACT FILE

Population: 64,000
Size: Bermuda's total land area, consisting of 181 islands and islets, is 34 km (21 miles) long and 2km (1 mile) wide.
Parishes: Nine – St George's, Smith's, Hamilton, Pembroke, Devonshire, Paget, Warwick, Southampton, Sandys.
Government: Self-governing British Overseas Territory, second oldest parliamentary democracy in the world.

Caribbean – that famed string of islands lies 1610km (1000 miles) to the southwest and Bermuda is closer to Nova Scotia – but it feels far more laid-back and welcoming than its First World facilities and global reputation for finance and insurance may suggest.

For many North American and European visitors the climate is sublime with cooling breezes to temper the worst of the summer heat and balmy winters that never see frost or snow. Bermuda is certainly no budget destination, but it does offer plenty for your money, including world-class beaches spread around the nine parishes. Incidentally, these take their names from the major investors, or adventurers, in the Bermuda Company who led the colonization of the islands in 1615. Initially the parishes were known as tribes, although this is a label that St George's, Hamilton, Smith's, Devonshire, Pembroke, Paget, Warwick, Southampton and Sandys have long since dispensed with. In addition, Bermuda wows visitors with an impressive galaxy of offshore reefs, as well as bountiful opportunities for water sports, numerous golf courses, hiking trails and plenty of opportunity for messing about in boats. Backing up its carefree leisure pursuits is a swathe of history in the town of St George – one of the British Empire's greatest and best-preserved legacies – as well as a scattering of fortifications dotted all around the islands, harking back to the days when man first scrambled ashore on these idyllic islands in the Gulf Stream. Despite Bermuda's bijou size there are still tracts of land where you can have your own Robinson Crusoe experience.

THE LAND

Bermuda is a British colony located 946km (570 miles) off the east coast of Cape Hatteras in North Carolina, 1284km (774 miles) southeast of New York and around 1610km (1000 miles) northeast of the Caribbean. This completely isolated territory is in fact a collection of approximately 181 islands and islets, of which just 20 are inhabited. The main islands – St George's Island, St David's Island, Bermuda Island, Ireland Island (North and South), Somerset Island, Boaz Island and Watford Island – are linked by causeways and bridges and they are often referred to simply as 'The Island'.

The formation of this collection of islands (The Bermudas) is believed to have begun around 100 million years ago, with the eruptions of an underwater volcano (which has been extinct for almost 33 million years). Scientists believe that the volcano's limestone cap (the islands that you can see today) took a comparatively short 1.6 million years to form. During this time the sea level varied by roughly 150m (500ft), a variation that was caused by the melting and refreezing of the polar icecaps. During cold periods Bermuda's visible landmass stretched to 1000km² (390 sq miles), receding to 30km² (12 sq miles) when the caps melted and the sea level rose. When sea levels were low Bermuda's reef was exposed, allowing the wind to deposit coral sand on the islands to form sand dunes. Over time soil accumulated on the dunes, which was in turn transformed into limestone by the rain. Tireless Atlantic winds then beat the dunes down to a flatter level, which forms the

CLIMATE

Bermuda is a small island without any real climatic differences between the parishes. The warmest months are June–August when the air temperature can approach 30°C (86°F); high humidity (80–85%) during these months can make the summer season very hot. In May, September and October daytime temperatures are in the low to mid 20s, while December to April are the coldest months, with the mercury hovering around 18–20°C (64–68°F). The sea is at its warmest between May and October, but it is warm enough for a dip at any time of year.

Below: *The tranquillity of one of Warwick's pristine South Shore beaches.*

Above: *A distinctive pink Bermuda bus leaving the grounds of the Grotto Bay Hotel.*

islands' territory today, leaving Bermuda a landmass of around 56km² (22 sq miles).

Climate
Air Temperature and Humidity

Sharing the same latitude as Atlanta, Bermuda has a much milder climate than it has any right to, as the Gulf Stream blesses it with year-round air temperatures that oscillate between 16°C and 27°C (61 and 81°F). In essence these subtropical islands only have two seasons: spring and summer. From December to April average daytime temperatures hover around 18°C (64°F), rising to the low to mid-20s in May, June, October and November. The hottest months in Bermuda are July–September when temperatures stay in the high 20s, but can reach 30°C (86°F).

Many islanders argue that it is not the temperature but the humidity that really delineates Bermuda's climate, with the humidity between June and August reaching up to 85%; the humidity in May is also high at around 80%, but this falls to 70–75% during the rest of the year.

Sea Temperature

The majority of Bermudians and foreigners living and working on the islands will only swim in the sea between the mid-May and mid-October, when sea temperatures are 20°C (68°F) or above. With water temperatures staying at around 20°C (68°F) in November before falling to 19°C (66°F) in December and 18°C (64°F) between January and April, the sea is, however, warm enough to swim in at any time of year.

HURRICANE FABIAN

Many an Atlantic hurricane has swished past nearby causing minor structural damage and instilling in Bermudians a certain sense of complacency. This was shattered in 2003 when the category three Hurricane Fabian smacked Bermuda with a direct hit that devastated two hotels (the Southampton and Sonesta), tore up sections of the South Road, closed the airport for a number of days and tragically left four islanders dead. Today hurricane tracking is a serious business.

BERMUDA	J	F	M	A	M	J	J	A	S	O	N	D
AVERAGE TEMP. °C	18	17	18	19	22	25	27	27	26	24	21	19
AVERAGE TEMP. °F	64.4	62.6	64.4	66.2	71.6	77	80.6	80.6	78.8	75.2	69.8	66.2
RAINFALL mm	120	110	100	80	70	120	110	120	120	160	100	110
RAINFALL in	5.0	4.3	3.9	3.1	2.7	5.0	4.3	5.0	5.0	6.2	3.9	4.3

Precipitation

As you might expect, these tiny and remote islands isolated in the Atlantic see a fair amount of rain. There is no clearly defined rainy season, with monthly precipitation averaging around 110mm (4.5 in). Rainfall, though, mostly takes the form of quickly passing showers. May is generally the driest month with just over 70mm (2.7in) of rain, while October, with an average precipitation of 160mm (6.6in), is the wettest month.

Hurricanes

In September 2003 **Hurricane Fabian** (see panel, page 8) swept though the islands causing $300 million of damage and claiming four lives, an event which made many Bermudians much more storm-aware. The majority of the Atlantic hurricanes, however, simply pass Bermuda by, subjecting it to little more than high winds, with **Hurricane Emily** in 1987 being the last hurricane to hit the islands before Fabian. The official Atlantic hurricane season lasts for the six months between June and November, though a December hurricane, **Epsilon**, circled the waters to the east of Bermuda in early December 2005.

Fauna and Flora
Plants, Shrubs and Trees

Trees, shrubs, plants and flowers from all over the globe thrive in Bermuda's subtropical climate. The Botanical Gardens in Paget (see pages 90–98) are the best place to

NOT THE CARIBBEAN!

If you want to severely irritate a local, suggest that Bermuda lies in the Caribbean, an unforgivable mistake as it actually lies closer to Nova Scotia. It is not particularly close to Miami either (another popular misconception) – being closer as the crow flies to New York City. It is, though, much nearer to Florida and the Caribbean in temperature in winter than either Nova Scotia or New York.

A CAVER'S DREAM

There is more to subterranean Bermuda than just the famous Crystal and Fantasy Caves. In fact Bermuda is said to boast the highest concentration of limestone caves in the world with hundreds of caves, everything from tiny gaps one person would struggle to squeeze into, through to grand caverns that you can walk around taking in the impressive stalactites and stalagmites as you go. Some locals believe that all of the caves are linked and scuba divers have managed to dive down one cave, struggle through a limestone web and emerge in a completely different location.

Left: A Red Admiral butterfly in the Butterfly Garden at the Botanical Gardens in Paget.

Above: *Lush vegetation with sub tropical palms vaulting towards a typically clear blue sky.*

learn about the different species grown in the territory. Only around 5% of what you see growing in Bermuda is indigenous, although around 3000 species are believed to have inhabited the island long before human beings. The **Bermudiana** (a member of the iris family identifiable by its tiny blue flowers), **olivewood bark**, **sword ferns** and the **palmetto**, which was commonly used to make thatch roofs for Bermuda's early houses, are among the islands' native flora.

Bermuda's most famous natural resident is the **Bermuda cedar**, with this hard-wearing wood traditionally used to construct houses (in 1687 around 96% of the homes on the island were made of wood), furniture, boats and shipping crates. Cedar wood was also used for fuel, while the tree's berries were used to make berry beer. In 1942, however, disaster struck this hardy indigenous tree, when scale insects that were accidentally introduced to Bermuda began to kill the trees – over the next decade or so the Bermuda cedar was virtually eradicated.

The rapid demise of the Bermuda cedar resulted in the importation of **Australian whistling pines** (now regarded as invasive), **Surinam cherry**, **Norfolk pines** and more exotic plants like **geraniums**, **oleander**, **hibiscus** and **prickly pear**. Fortunately the majority of the flora that has been introduced to Bermuda from overseas doesn't upset the islands' ecological balance too much; however, the **Brazilian pepper tree** (which sports attractive red seeds in the winter) spreads far too rapidly, while plants growing in close proximity to the **Chinese fan palm** slowly die. A number of the trees imported to the islands have become endemic, developing characteristics unique to Bermuda; these include the **wax myrtle** and the **southern hackberry**.

Mammals and Amphibians

Bermuda's geographical location and its evolution in deep waters means that few animals live on the islands, and those that do – **rats**, **mice**, **dogs**, **cats**, and **cows** – were brought to the islands by human settlers. The tiny **skink lizard** is Bermuda's only indigenous reptile.

Birds

Bermuda is a haven for ornithologists, with the **gray catbird**, **northern cardinal** and **Bermuda white-eyed vireo** (known locally as the chick of the village) among its native birds. One indigenous bird that you are not likely to see is the **Bermuda petrel** or **cahow** which, until it was rediscovered in 1951, was believed to have become extinct in the early 17th century. Introduced from Trinidad in 1957, the ubiquitous **kiskadee** has become naturalized, as have **starlings**.

Bermuda is also on the migratory routes of species as diverse as the **common yellow throat**, **barn swallows**, **common snipes**, **killdeer**, **mourning doves**, **ground doves**, **ducks**, **herons** and **grebes**. There are few natural spaces where the birds are able to go, but these include the nature reserves at Spittal Pond, Warwick Pond and Paget Marsh. Meanwhile the mudflats around Flatts Village provide temporary respite for migrating shore birds including various types of **sandpiper** and **plovers**.

BERMUDIAN SKINK

Bermuda boasts its own native lizard, the skink or rock lizard, which is so highly revered locally that residents are actively encouraged to 'make their gardens more skink friendly'; it even has its own website (www.bermudaskink.com). This unique non-climbing lizard, which originally came to Bermuda courtesy of the Gulf Stream, is usually heard and not seen as it scurries away from human contact into the undergrowth.

Below: *Since they first arrived from Trinidad back in the 1950s the distinctive yellow and black kiskadees have become a very common sight in Bermuda.*

THE BERMUDA TRIANGLE

Strange lights and spinning compasses were reported in the waters around Bermuda as early as the voyage of Christopher Columbus in 1492. Over the centuries the 804,500km (500,000 mile) triangle between Bermuda, Miami and Puerto Rico, which plunges at points to almost 10km (6 miles) deep, has always been associated with strange disappearances. Sturdy frigates, entire freighters and even a whole squadron of US Air Force bombers (and the tracking plane sent to find them) have all disappeared without a trace. Myriad theories abound about the source of the weird events, from time warps and UFOs through to giant sea squids, but today the Bermuda Triangle still very much remains a mystery.

Marine Life

Thanks to the Gulf Stream Bermuda boasts the most northerly coral reef and the most northerly mangrove swamps in the world. Scientists believe that Bermuda has around 100,000 native species of marine life, with most of these originating in the Caribbean and North America. The North Lagoon, which stretches from the north shore to the outer reef, is home to a variety of reef and shoreline fish, with **Atlantic parrotfish** (of which there are 14 varieties), **killifish** and **Bermuda bream** commonly found in Bermuda's waters. The parrotfish earned their name from the long beaks that they use to scrape seaweed from the reef. Alongside other grazers they help control algae and aid the conversion of coral rock to sediment. **Spotted eagle rays, pompano, grunts, sea cucumber** and **bonefish** inhabit the lagoon's sandy floor. The lush sea grass on the lagoon base is also home to **crabs**, **clams** and **turtles**. The Bermudian crustacean that you are most likely to encounter is the great land crab, which inhabits the area around the south shore beaches. The female crabs can grow quite large, with the biggest found to date measuring 30 cm (1ft) from her right to left; however, sightings are uncommon. Another rare species that you will definitely not see as they live beneath the sandy lagoon floor is the calico clam.

These shellfish almost became extinct back in the 1970s. It has been illegal to harvest or eatcalico clams since 1978; a rearing project in Harrington Sound is seeking to increase their numbers. In March and April Bermuda is visited by migrating **sperm whales** and **humpback whales**, with a number of local tour operators, including Fantasea Bermuda (www.fantasea.bm), organizing whale-watching tours at this time of year.

Another sea dweller that visitors and locals alike need to keep an eye open for is the **Portuguese man-of-war** – a poisonous jellyfish with a purple-tinged dome and long tentacles which can issue a very painful sting. The jellyfish is most prevalent during spring and early summer.

HISTORY IN BRIEF
Early Discovery
Bermuda first appeared on the map in the Spanish atlas *Legatio Babylonica* in 1511, although most historians agree that it was discovered sometime between 1503 and 1506 by Spanish explorer **Juan de Bermúdez** (hence its modern-day name), who by all accounts was less than impressed with the islands' charms, nicknaming them *Islas Demonios*, or **Devil's Isles**.

It is unlikely that Bermúdez and his ship *La Garza* (Heron) ever landed in Bermuda, with the history books suggesting that the captain and his crew strove to avoid the treacherous coral reef that fringed the islands and had caused other Spanish ships to sink. The eerie bird calls and the sound of squealing wild hogs, which Bermúdez mistakenly believed were the screams of tortured human souls, undoubtedly helped keep him away.

There is some suggestion that Bermuda may have been discovered almost a thousand years earlier by **St Brendan**, who is said to have miraculously sailed here aboard a much smaller wooden boat, although historians as yet have not been able to prove or disprove the theory.

Shipwrecks
The next record of human habitation of the islands dates back to 1543 when a Spanish ship is thought to have run aground on the coral reefs to the north of the islands near Spittal Pond (*see page 69*), although some accounts claim the shipwreck was that of a Portuguese vessel bound for the Dominican Republic. All of the crew are believed to have survived, with the 30 sailors coming ashore to build a new ship before continuing with their voyage; the British later found evidence of their stay and

Above: *Gun muzzle overlooking the Atlantic from Fort St Catherine at the northeast tip of Bermuda.* **Opposite:** *Bermuda Aquarium allows visitors to the islands to get close to the tropical fish living in the surrounding waters without getting wet.*

WHAT'S IN A NAME?

Nowhere in the world as small can have had so many names. Bermuda has been the 'Islands of Devils' to the Spanish, 'Virginiola' to the first British castaways (either in honour of their intended destination or their recently deceased Virgin Queen) and 'Somers' Isles' after the man credited with first settling Bermuda (sometimes spelt 'Summer's Isles' as a weather related pun). Today Bermuda is 'The Island', 'The Islands', 'De Rock' or 'The Mainland'.

Above: *A reconstruction of Sir Somers' ship, the* Deliverance.

gave the area its current name, Spanish Point. Towards the latter half of the 16th century French ships are also thought to have fallen victim to Bermuda's shallow coral reefs, perpetuating its notorious reputation.

The Arrival of the British

Over a hundred years after Juan de Bermúdez edged warily past Bermuda, the *Sea Venture*, captained by the accomplished but rather unlucky **Sir George Somers**, ran into a ferocious storm to the east of Bermuda, which sent them way off course and separated his flagship from the rest of the fleet. Spotting land on the third day he steered the battered ship to the safety of the islands only to crash into the shallow reef; however, all 150 of its crew made it ashore.

The *Sea Venture* had been part of a convoy heading to the British colony of Jamestown in Virginia in order to provide urgently needed supplies. A man of his word, Somers was determined to complete his mission and the crew spent the best part of a year constructing two new vessels – the aptly named Patience and Deliverance – from the cedar trees that grew all over

Bermuda, in order to complete their journey to the Jamestown colony in Virginia. During their stay they conquered the Spanish fear of devils, and records show that they enjoyed a rich harvest of fruit, fish and birds.

In Jamestown Somers discovered a colony that was far from flourishing. In fact it had been virtually decimated and was soon abandoned, so the British ships headed back to the much more welcoming arms of Bermuda. The return visit met with more misfortune for Somers as he succumbed to a heart attack in 1610, with his heart and other remains famously left in St George (*see* panel, page 45) and the rest of him pickled in alcohol and shipped back to his native England.

Early Settlers

In 1612 the first intentional British settlers, under the governance of **Richard Moore**, who was employed by the **Virginia Company**, arrived in Bermuda aboard *The Plough*, naming the islands **Somers' Isles** and its new capital St George in honour of the man who established Britain's Bermuda connection. The eight main islands were divided into nine parishes, which were named after the Virginia Company's stockholders and still exist today.

EAST AND WEST?

Look at Bermuda on a map and some Bermuda virgins are tempted to suggest it runs from St George's Parish in the north towards Sandys in the south. Don't try telling that to a local as they are firmly convinced their fish hook shaped islands scoop from St George's in the east to Sandys in the west and often divide their islands up in conversation between the 'West End' and the 'East End'. The truth may actually be a bit of both as Bermuda really runs from northeast to south-west, but for convenience you are best just sticking with the often compass-challenging local version.

Below: *The now redundant stocks on King's Square in St George.*

Opposite: *The stately Hamilton Princess, Bermuda's most historic hotel named after Princess Louise who opened this grand old dame in 1885.*

The colonists soon realized that the island, despite its plentiful wood and food, did not have enough other natural resources to support them and began to import things from abroad, trading with tobacco, oil, pearls and ambergris. The latter, a whale product used in the manufacture of perfume, was occasionally washed up on Bermuda's shores, though perhaps not in the quantities that the settlers led the Virginia Company back in England to believe.

In 1616 white settlers brought black slaves (mainly from Africa) to the islands for the first time, while the first session of the Bermuda Parliament was held in St Peter's Church in St George in 1620. Bermuda grew quickly and its settlers soon became annoyed with the interference of the Virginia Company, managing to break free in 1684 to become a British colony.

Accommodation

Wherever you choose to stay in Bermuda it will not be cheap (it is hard to find somewhere to stay for much less than $100 a night), although many places discount their rates substantially between November and March. Bermudians are allowed to take up to four paying guests without applying for a license, although word of mouth is generally the only way to find out who offers this type of service. It is normally wise to book more affordable accommodation in advance.

Bermuda and the USA

Over time this isolated British colony formed strong trading links with the USA, although the relationship wasn't always an easy one. Tensions grew on a number of fronts and during the 1812 Chesapeake Bay Campaign, British ships sailed from Bermuda to attack the White House and Washington DC. After this British assault, American privateers (a legal form of piracy) were quick to exact a crippling revenge on Bermuda, as they looted the colony's ships. Slavery was another bone of contention, while Britain had passed The Abolition of Slavery Act in 1833 (the slave trade itself had been outlawed years earlier in 1807), with Bermuda ending slavery in 1834, the USA persisted with the slave trade until 1865.

The American Civil War (1861–65) actually proved itself a boon to Bermuda's economy. It became a base for Confederate blockade-

HISTORICAL CALENDAR

1503–06 Spanish sailors first sight Bermuda.
1511 Bermuda appears on the map for the first time.
1610 George Somers is shipwrecked in Bermuda.
1612 First British colonists arrive.
1616 Slaves are brought to the island.
1812 Bermudian ships are

targeted by American privateers after the Chesapeake Bay Campaign.
1834 Slavery is abolished.
1884 First holiday resort opens.
1968 Universal suffrage is granted.
1995 Bermudians reject independence from Great Britain.

runners who ran valuable cotton from the south to be traded with the British. This was dangerous but lucrative work and St George in particular prospered. In the aftermath of the Civil War the USA put its troubles behind it and emerged as a major economic and military power, seriously worrying the British for whom Bermuda, along with Halifax in Nova Scotia, was a key western Atlantic strategic hub. A web of fortifications (many of which you can still see today) sprouted around Bermuda as British paranoia reached epidemic levels.

A New World Order

The 20th century saw the geopolitical position change again, with the USA becoming a key ally for Britain in both world wars and American troops being stationed on Bermuda, where they stayed on until the 1990s. After World War II, American influence grew in Bermuda and progress was made with black and women's rights, with women getting the vote in 1944 and a strong black empowerment lobby emerging in the 1950s.

Modernday Bermuda

Bermuda has come a long way in a relatively short time. Today it is a popular tourist destination, especially with North Americans, who come here to escape the ravages of their winter. It has also emerged as a major global finance and insurance hub, with a staggering annual GDP of over $4 billion, making it one of the richest places in the world. The key question when it comes to Bermuda's future is its relationship with Britain. Its status as a British Overseas Territory remains the subject of much local debate, with a referendum in the 1990s showing most voters were happy to stay with the status quo. In the

EMERGENCY IN BERMUDA

The calm of Bermudian political life was shattered in 1973 when governor Sir Richard Sharples was gunned down along with his bodyguard in the grounds of Government House, less than a year after the Commissioner of Police had met the same fate. As tensions rose, two convicted black criminals, Buch Burrows and Larry Tacklyn, were marched through the justice system and hanged for the crime. Riots exploded on the streets of Hamilton. There was an arson attack on a tourist hotel and a state of emergency was declared.

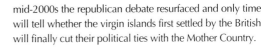

Bermuda is nothing if not conservative and it took a while to catch up with the rest of the world when it came to women's rights. Finally as World War II came to a close in 1944 Bermudian women who owned property were given the right to vote for the first time. Some locals do complain that Bermuda is still very much a male dominated world.

mid-2000s the republican debate resurfaced and only time will tell whether the virgin islands first settled by the British will finally cut their political ties with the Mother Country.

GOVERNMENT

Bermuda is a British Overseas Territory, which has been granted internal self-government. It exercises a system of democratic rule with separate executive, legislative and judicial branches. Bermuda's executive comprises the islands' Premier, the Hon W Alexander Scott (who has held the post since July 2003), and the Governor, Sir John Vereker, who is the Queen's representative in Bermuda and is largely a figurehead. The legislature is composed of the Senate and the House of Assembly, with the former having 11 democratically elected members and the latter 36 members. All Bermudians aged 18 years and over are eligible to vote; however, universal suffrage wasn't granted until 1968. In the 2003 elections the Progressive Labour Party (PLP) won 52% of the vote (22 seats) and the United Bermuda Party (UBP) 48% of the vote (14 seats). Bermuda's next election is slated for July 2008.

Independence
In 1995 a public referendum saw almost three-quarters of Bermudians reject independence from Great Britain. Despite this, independence remains a hot topic, which regularly features on the pages of Bermuda's daily newspaper, the *Royal Gazette*.

Below: *Bermuda's un-mistakeable red flag adorned with a Union Jack and Bermudian coat of arms flying proudly from Fort Scaur.*

Bermuda's Flag
Bermuda's flag has a red background with a Union Jack, which occupies a quarter of the flag, superimposed onto the top left-hand corner. The right half of the flag contains the Bermudian coat of arms, which comprises a white shield featuring a red lion holding another shield depicting Sir George Somers' ship, the *Sea Venture*, being shipwrecked off Bermuda.

ECONOMY

Bermuda's citizens enjoy one of the highest per capita incomes in the world, which is incredible when you consider its compact size. In 2004 the islands' GDP was $4.4 billion, while its per capita purchasing power parity was estimated to be $36,000. The economy also benefits from low inflation and favourable tax conditions that see employers pay the bulk of the employment tax. Unemployment is low (around 4%), although almost a fifth of the territory's population are classed as poor. Underpinning Bermuda's booming economy are a raft of companies providing financial services, including rein-surance, to businesses around the globe.

Another key component of the islands' economy is tourism, with almost 483,000 tourist arrivals in 2004. More important than the income generated by tourism is its pivotal role in Bermuda's employment market. The vast majority of the islands' tourist trade (85%) comes from North America, with short flight times and the agreeable climate making it an attractive year-round destination for this market. Service industries generate around 90% of Bermuda's GDP. Due to its small size, the lack of a natural fresh water supply and the relative absence of industry, practically everything that Bermudians use has to be imported (bananas, citrus fruits and other vegetables are grown on the islands) and this in turn makes costs high.

Above: *Multicultural Bermuda on display on Hamilton's Front Street.*

THE PEOPLE

Bermuda is unusual in that it does not have an indigenous population; the earliest settlers were the British colonists who arrived in 1612. In 1617 they brought the first black settlers to the islands as slaves. In 1849 Portuguese agricultural workers arrived in Bermuda and their descendents still comprise a small proportion of Bermudian society. Today around 61% of the population are of black African origin, with the remaining 39% mainly white.

FINDING 'MR RIGHT'

The claim in the British *Daily Express* in November 2005 that Bermuda was now the world's top place to find Mr Right was met with a mixture of mild surprise and utter bewilderment on the islands. The thinking went that 'Thanks to its status as one of the world's tax havens Bermuda has become a prime hunting ground for single women. Their target: the hundreds of male lawyers and accountants who have been shipped in to the Island to keep their companies' accounts in order'.

TYING THE BERMUDIAN KNOT

Bermuda, with its pink sands, hideaway hotels and gorgeous sunsets, has to be one of the most romantic places in the world to get married. About 23,000 couples a year tie the knot in Bermuda. To get legally married couples have to file and pay for a 'Notice of Intended Marriage' at least four weeks before the big day. When a marriage licence is subsequently issued they have three months in which to tie the knot.

Bermuda is a multidenominational society with around 25% of the population belonging to the Anglican Church and 15% to the Catholic Church. A further 30% of the population are Protestant or other Christian, with 12% of this group being African Methodist Episcopal. Bermuda also has a mosque for its Muslim population.

Traditions

On the surface Bermuda is a modern society, with little visible evidence of a traditional way of life. Some traditional practices are, however, brought back to life during Bermuda's festivals and during tourist re-enactments.

West African Traditions

Bermuda's African heritage is at its most prominent in Gombey dancing. This tribal dance has its origins in West Africa, with 17th-century slaves bringing it to the islands with them; in fact the word *Gombey* comes from the Bantu word for rhythm. Today it has evolved to incorporate a number of influences including that of the West Indies, British military bands and native Americans, who are the inspiration for the elaborate and brightly coloured costumes, which are supposed to be evocative of exotic birds. Many of the dancers wear grotesque masks. Traditionally the Gombey is performed on Boxing Day (26 December) and New Year's Day; this is symbolic of the respite briefly granted in the past to slaves on these days. Today the Gombey can also be seen on Easter Monday and is danced throughout the year for tourists. Historically the dancers are male, and it is traditional for a father to pass his skills on to his son.

Below: *A Gombey band performing in Hamilton. The tradition of the father teaching his son the dance starts at a young age.*

British Traditions

Many of Bermuda's hotels observe the English custom of **afternoon tea**, which is typically served between 15:00 and 17:00. At some establishments it is provided free of charge. Traditionally this indulgent snack comprises cucumber sandwiches, scones with jam and cream, and tea. It is not unusual, though, to find a more diverse sandwich selection, accompanied by a variety of cakes, herbal teas and coffee.

Cricket

The first cricket match played on Bermudian soil is thought to have taken place back in 1844. In the years since, the sport has evolved into something of a national institution, with the two-day July holiday given over to the Cup Match. Despite the islanders' passion for the sport, Bermuda's cricket heroes have never done particularly well on the international stage; however, in 2005 they qualified for the 2007 Cricket World Cup, their first time.

Above: Bermudians exhibiting their passion for cricket in a spirited afternoon game.

Bagpipes

In the 18th century British soldiers from Scotland and Northern Ireland introduced the bagpipes to Bermuda, and the islanders have long since fallen in love with them – the islands boast their own pipe band. The biggest pipe events are the Beating Retreat Ceremony, the Queen's Official Birthday Parade (June) and Remembrance Day (*see* panel, page 29). The Beating Retreat Ceremony is re-enacted for tourists at various intervals throughout the year, and is basically a call for soldiers to return to barracks. There is also a weekly bagpipe rendition (the Skirling Ceremony) against the spectacular backdrop of Hamilton Fort on Mondays from November to March.

CRICKET CRAZY

The biggest event of the year for many Bermudians is the Cup Match at the end of July, a tradition dating back to 1902. This two-day extravaganza, which centres around a highly competitive cricket match between teams from St George (dark blue and light blue) and Somerset (red and blue), takes place on Emancipation Day and Somers' Day.

Portuguese Traditions

The Portuguese components of Bermuda's cultural history are harder to discern, and are most evident in the food, through dishes like spicy red bean soup. The territory does have a Portuguese Cultural Association, whose dance troupe participates in the Bermuda Day celebrations (*see* panel, page 126).

Bermudian Traditions
Kite Flying

If you are lucky enough to be in Bermuda on Good Friday you will see a variety of colourful kites being flown from beaches and parks all over the islands. Kite flying is also a popular pastime on blustery days. The practice of kite flying has Christian roots, when kites with wooden crosses (symbolic of the crucifixion) were flown in celebration of the life of Jesus Christ.

Moongates

Although moongates originally came from China, they have been an important part of Bermudian culture for almost 150 years. Local legend has it that a Bermudian sea captain, who had been so enamoured by the notion of moongates during a voyage to China, set about designing and building his own upon his return home.

Below: *Atlantic sea breezes blowing across the islands are perfect for kite flying.*

Other Bermudians liked his idea and it quickly caught on. Today you can find moongates, made with Bermuda stone, in a number of places, particularly at hotels and the entrances to gardens, due to the symbolism that they have come to acquire. If you pass through a moongate people will tell you that it will bring you luck, peace and everlasting happiness, while others claim that any wish made beneath the arch will come true. It is perhaps unsurprising that many newlyweds (both locals and tourists) exchange their marriage vows beneath a moongate.

Food

When people talk about Bermudian cuisine they are often referring to a style of cooking, due to the fact that much of the islands' produce has to be imported. You will, however, find locally caught fish on the menu in many of Bermuda's restaurants, including tuna, spiny lobster, wahoo, mahi mahi and snapper.

Codfish Cakes

Fish is a key ingredient in one of the most Bermudian of dishes, salted codfish, which is traditionally served with bananas and eaten for breakfast on Sundays. Codfish breakfasts, which often take the form of fishcakes, are available in many hotel dining rooms and restaurants around the islands. Avocado is another popular accompaniment. On Good Friday codfish cakes are eaten with hot cross buns. The fishcakes themselves are made with cod, mashed potato, egg, onion, pepper and flour.

Fish Chowder

Fish chowder is one of Bermuda's national dishes and features on almost every menu; it probably originated in Britain and came to the islands with the first colonists. This spicy soup has evolved over time, with a dash of dark spicy rum and sherry peppers lending it a uniquely Bermudian flavour. The basic ingredients also include fish stock, fish, bacon fat, vegetables and spices.

Pies

Many of the savoury pies typically considered Bermudian – cassava, sweet potato and mussel – also

Above: *Room service breakfast at the Pink Beach Club, served in the private garden overlooking the Atlantic.*

DINE AROUND SCHEME

Hotels that belong to the Bermuda Collection – **Cambridge Beaches**, **The Reefs**, **Pompano Beach Club** and **Coco Reefs** – operate a 'Dine Around' scheme, which allows a certain number of guests who are staying on a Modified American Plan (MAP) basis (which includes breakfast and an evening meal) to dine at the restaurants of other member properties without any additional charge. Diners must of course cover their own transport costs and pay for their own drinks.

BERMUDA HONEY

Honey production in Bermuda is, as you would expect, on a comparatively small scale. That said, there are no fewer than 24 beekeepers on the islands. Visitors can get to grips with the territory's beekeeping traditions and uncover myriad fascinating facts, such as that bees' wings flap more than 11,000 times per minute, at the Bermuda Bee Museum and apiaries of Randolph Furbert Junior, which is located at the Honey House, Chartwell Apiaries, Bailey's Bay, tel: 799-3061.

originate from overseas, but are mainstays in restaurants and on household tables throughout the territory today. **Cassava pie** comes from Central and South America, but was brought to Bermuda by West African slaves. Eggs, chicken, sugar, pork and nutmeg are just some of the ingredients that are used alongside cassava flour (the ground edible root of a woody shrub) to make this savoury pie. A less fattening alternative comes in the form of **sweet potato pie**, where this root vegetable is blended with a variety of herbs and spices. Mussels steamed and mixed with various vegetables and seasoning and served in a pastry crust also feature on Bermudian menus in the form of **mussel pie**. At one time locals even harvested their own mussels in Harrington Sound.

Bread

Bermudians have also incorporated various breads into their culinary repertoire, including **corn bread**, which orig-

inated in Mexico and then spread to various countries around the globe before arriving in Bermuda. During the 19th century another bread recipe came to the territory, this time in the form of the sweet **Easter bread** (originally from British West Indies), which is decorated with coloured eggs.

Honey

Since the importation of bees in the early 17th century, Bermudians have turned their hand to beekeeping, with the main harvests being in June–July and September–October. According to Bermudian folklore, honey produced by their bees is an aphrodisiac.

Drinks

Bermuda's microbrewery, the **North Rock Brewing Company** (*see* page 74), ensures that there is a beermaking tradition on the island, however, Bermuda is more renowned for its exotic cocktails, with any extension of hospitality frequently being accompanied by an offer of a **Rum Swizzle** or **Dark 'n' Stormy**. The former is a refreshing blend of dark rum (preferably the islands' own Gosling's Black Seal Rum) and fruit juices; the latter is made with dark spiced rum and ginger beer. Bermudians will tell you, however, that while the basic ingredients are the same, no two people make these signature tipples in the same way.

Sport and Recreation

The two most popular sports in Bermuda are cricket, which is played between April and September, and football, with matches taking place between October and April. The Bermudian love of cricket is most apparent in the two-day July Cup Match. Rugby, softball, bowling and tennis are also popular sports. Visitors to Bermuda, though, are more likely to pursue water sports like sailing, fishing, scuba diving, parasailing, jet-skiing and water-skiing. Yacht and power boat races also take place at frequent intervals during the summer.

WINTER DINE AROUND

This scheme, which operates from November to mid-April, allows you to dine at three of the restaurants in the Little Venice Group – Little Venice, L'Oriental, Harbourfront, La Trattoria, La Coquille, Fourways Inn, Lido Complex and Café Boulevard – for $120 per person.

GOLFERS' PARADISE

It may only be 56km² (22 sq miles) in area, but Bermuda manages to squeeze in no fewer than eight golf courses and one driving range. In the extreme east there is St George's with ultra exclusive Tucker's Point and Mid Ocean to the west across the water. Just east of Hamilton is the Ocean View course, while west of the capital are Belmont Hills and Riddell's Bay. Southampton Parish boasts the Fairmont Southampton Golf Club at the eponymous hotel, while further yet to the west is the Port Royal course and the Bermuda Golf Academy Driving Range.

Opposite: *Ginger beer – Bermuda's most popular soft drink.*
Left: *A golfer lining up a shot at the Port Royal Golf Course.*

Bermuda has eight golf courses, which is incredible when you consider that the islands measure just 56km² (22 sq miles). Most golfers are drawn to the lush links courses. Only three – Ocean View, Port Royal and St George's – are public courses; however, many hotels have agreements with the private courses and can often book a tee-off time for their guests.

The territory also has a strong equestrian tradition, and horse showjumping, dressage events and gymkhanas are popular spectator sports, with the biggest show being the Annual Exhibition (*see* page 126).

Above: *A sculpture by Desmond Hale Fountain.*

(see page 126).

CALENDAR OF MAJOR FESTIVALS

Bermuda Festival of the Performing Arts January/February.
Bermuda Kite Festival March/April.
Bermuda International Film Festival April.
Bermuda Music Festival October.
Bermuda Culinary Arts Festival November.

Art

When people think of Bermuda's artistic heritage they tend to focus on the internationally acclaimed artists – George Ault, Albert Gleizes, Winslow Homer and Andrew Wyeth – who have painted the islands, rather than on the achievements of Bermudian artists themselves. The territory does, however, have a rich artistic tradition that dates back to the mid-18th century. Some of the works that you are most likely to see as a visitor include the portraits of Bermudian landowners painted by the Englishman Joseph Blackburn (also known as Jonathan Blackburn), who spent two years in Bermuda between 1752 and 1754. Another portrait painter, John Green (who was also a judge), painted Bermudian portraits when he moved to the island and married Thomas Smith's daughter in the mid-18th century.

Green and his wife resided in Verdmont House and the artist's works are now part of the museum's collection (*see* page 72).

Another locally renowned artist is Lady Lefroy, who worked with watercolours to reproduce Bermuda's nature and wildlife during the 19th century. Towards the end of the century the fine art paintings of Susan Frith, Bessie Gray and Lucy Trott Watlington began to appear. The work of Thomas Driver, Edward James (whose true identity remains unknown), Charles Lloyd Tucker, Charles Zuill, the modernist painter Alfred Birdsey and Sheilagh Head (www.sheilaghhead.com) have also achieved critical acclaim in Bermuda. The watercolours of Lisa Quinn, Carole Holding, Jill Amos Raine and Diane Amos are popular tourist souvenirs. The Bermuda National Gallery (*see* page 37) is the best place to see Bermudian art.

Sculpture

One certainty of a visit to Bermuda is that you will come across the works of Desmond Hale Fountain (*see* panel, page 32). His monument to Sir George Somers is one of Bermuda's iconic attractions (*see* page 45). Visitors to the Bermuda Arts Centre in the Royal Naval Dockyard will also find the studio of wood sculptor, Chesley Trott.

Music

While Bermuda is not renowned for its music, many Bermudians are still passionate about music and exhibit diverse musical tastes that incorporate classical, pop and jazz alongside Caribbean calypso music and the more tribal sounds of the Gombey band. The islands' most famous musical daughter is Heather Nova, who was actually born Heather Frith in 1967. Heather left the islands when she was just a child and didn't fully realize her musical talent until 1990 when she released her first album, the then eponymous

THE UNINTENTIONAL RESIDENT

Setting sail from Liverpool, Edward K James certainly did not envisage living in Bermuda. However, when his troubled ship (the *Deliverance*) docked in the islands he appears to have made a snap decision to stay, making Bermuda his home from 1861 until he died, aged 57, in 1877. Soon after his arrival James continued to peddle his trade as an artist, selling paintings he completed aboard the *Deliverance* and working as a naval architect from 1862–65, when it seems he managed to get himself fired from an unpaid post.

Below: *A traditional band entertains guests with the rhythmic Gombey beat.*

Above: *An example of Bermudian Art Deco.*

Heather Frith. Since then the singer has enjoyed moderate success, primarily in the USA. Her other albums are titled *Glowstars*, *Blow*, *Oyster*, *Live from the Milky Way*, *Siren*, *South*, *Wonderlust* and *Storm*. Bermudians also herald the achievement of pop singer and concert promoter Eddie DeMello, who was actually born in the Azores.

Architecture

Bermuda's 17th-century settlers utilized the natural resources that they found in abundance around the islands to build their homes. As such, houses were typically timber frames made from the tough wood of the prolific Bermuda cedar – the frame was then filled in with daub (soil mixed with grass and straw) – with thatched roofs. By the 18th century Bermudians had begun to build their houses with stone, discovering that this stood up to fierce Atlantic storms much better, with the cedar wood being employed in shipbuilding instead. One of the earliest examples of a Bermudian stone building is the Carter House, which is located on St David's Island in St George's parish and dates back to the mid-17th century. Bermuda's most distinctive architectural feature are the roofs that top the pastel-hued houses and buildings. In the absence of any natural water source these roofs, which are triangular prisms created by a series of shallow walls, coated in a

NAMES OR NUMBERS

Look closely at local houses and you will notice that some don't seem to have a number, but instead just a name. Traditionally houses were demarcated with an unusual local twist that meant sometimes a married couple's surnames would be amalgamated to create a truly unique name. The government has been trying to institute a more systematic numbering system in recent years, which has worked to some extent in places like the City of Hamilton, but not so well on the fringes like St David's Island.

limestone wash and then painted white, are designed to catch the precious rainwater, which is then stored in the basement. It is not only the water-catching rooftops that are unique to Bermuda, but the houses themselves, and unlike much of the islands' food and culture they are not imported from anywhere else.

Another typical characteristic of Bermudian dwellings are their thick limestone walls; LImestone was readily available on the islands back in the 18th century, when it was virtually impossible and certainly prohibitively expensive to import construction materials. The pastel exteriors and colourful window shutters, which lend Bermudian houses their unique charm, are reflections on the sunny outlook of the islanders. The balconies exist of course to take advantage of Bermuda's balmy weather and the stunning sea views afforded to many islanders, while the cuboid chimneys are an ever present reminder of the fact that Bermudian homes do not have central heating, but are warmed on colder days by fires burning in the hearth.

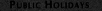

PUBLIC HOLIDAYS

New Year's Day • 1 January
Good Friday • March/April
Labour Day • 1 May
Bermuda Day • 24 May
(public holiday marked with land and water races, a half-marathon, and a parade)
Queen's Birthday • June
(marked by a military parade)
Emancipation Day & Somers' Day • July
Remembrance Day • 11 November
Christmas Day • 25 December
Boxing Day • 26 December

Below: *Typically colourful Bermudian architecture.*

2
City of Hamilton

To many locals Hamilton is simply 'town', the only real working town (officially a city) on the island. It is the place where you come to change buses, catch a ferry, do your shopping, meet friends and go out. Hamilton boasts a real buzz, with busy streets that actually need traffic lights, rushing office workers (many of them sporting Bermuda shorts in summer) and a sprinkling of pavement cafés and restaurants where tourists and locals alike relax and take in the scene.

Hamilton is named in honour of Sir Henry Hamilton, the man who proclaimed it Bermuda's new capital in 1815 at the expense of St George, though Hamilton was only recognized as a city after the cathedral, that Queen Victoria insisted was built first, was finished in 1897. It is very much a planned settlement, with a neat grid of streets rising up the hillside from the waterfront boulevard of Front Street. Among the busy shops and businesses are a flurry of churches, art galleries and museums that add a bit of depth to the modern face of Hamilton, and there are also a number of green spaces where you can relax on a sunny day.

St George may be prettier and there are no great beaches in Hamilton, but every visitor to Bermuda will at least pass through at some point and it is well worth taking some time to explore the main sights, which are dotted around the city in a compact space that can easily be explored on foot.

DON'T MISS

*** Fort Hamilton: stunning views over the city, harbour and the Great Sound.
*** Johnnie Barnes: his warm welcome sets the mood for the rest of the day.
*** Government Buildings: explore the powerhouses of Bermuda's government.
*** Front Street: indulge in a spot of shopping, watch the frenetic traffic from a raised terrace, or simply look out over the harbour.
** Churches of Church Street: Bermuda's Christian heritage.
** Parks: find a tranquil spot away from the roar of traffic.

Opposite: *The Cathedral of the Most Holy Trinity.*

Fort Hamilton ★★★

The best view of Hamilton is well worth the hike. On this hilly bluff the sturdy fortifications offer a bird's-eye view of the city streets stretching out below and boats bobbing in the harbour. The product of British paranoia in the 19th century, this expansive fort bristles with stone walls, arms stores and big guns. You can also duck down into the old moat that lies below the drawbridge you walk across on the way in, where a jungle-like oasis awaits, awash with lush vegetation – but beware of shady characters skulking around with their beer bottles, especially out of season.

Look out also for the underground tunnels that you can enter, which were constructed to help store the fort's ammunition in a safe place. The most atmospheric time to visit is at midday on Mondays in winter when the skirl of bagpipes haunts the fort as part of the 'Skirling Ceremony', a colourful tourist-orientated swish of kilts and music performed by the **Bermuda Islands Pipe Band**.

Johnnie Barnes ★★★

This oddball individual is something very peculiar to Bermuda. Every morning, no matter what the weather, for over two decades, this indefatigable figure has

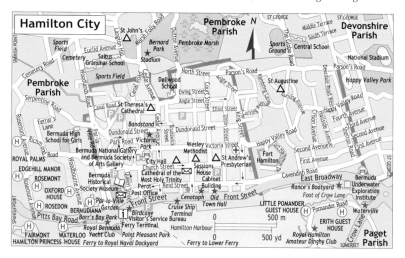

been welcoming rush-hour commuters to Hamilton with a smile, a wave and a friendly greeting.

Even before he retired from his job as a bus mechanic, he used to come and stand by the busy road junction before work. Now in his 80s, Johnnie shows no signs of suffering from his years spent inhaling exhaust fumes, and he now has a permanent presence on the junction, thanks to the statue of him (sculpted by local talent Desmond Hale Fountain) that stands as a solid reminder of the man who is such a great advert for ultra-friendly Bermuda.

Front Street ***
Always the hub of city life, Front Street can be lost amongst a crush of mopeds and buses, but take a step back and you can admire the fine old buildings, many bedecked in pastel colours and sporting raised verandas, that peer out over the harbour. These graceful old dames are a much-needed counterweight to the phalanx of glass and steel office buildings that have risen in recent years to accompany the boom in the finance and insurance industries. Snare a seat on the veranda of one of the pubs or restaurants and just take in the scene.

BEST BUYS

If you are looking for value for money when it comes to gifts then bear the following in mind. Alcohol is much cheaper when it is bought duty free at the airport. Perfume and cosmetics are also good buys and generally cheaper than UK prices; the range on offer at the airport is, however, limited and you'd be better off buying these from the shops on Front Street in the City of Hamilton.

Below: *The pastel-hued historic buildings of bustling Front Street.*

HONKING HORNS

When you first dare to ride a moped the constant beeping of horns can be a little disconcerting. As you approach a blind bend there is a loud honk, but far from being a truck about to zoom at you on the wrong side of the road it is just a local saying hello to his mate. Honking the horn as a greeting is officially illegal in Bermuda, but no one has told the locals, as it is used instead of a wave, whether you are aforementioned truck or bus driver or even a moped rider.

Below: *The poignant Cenotaph Memorial remembers Bermudians who lost their lives in both world wars.*

Retail addicts meanwhile can buy their supplies of Outerbridge's sauces, Gosling's Black Seal Rum and Bermuda Rum Cake in the shops that line Front Street. You can easily spend a whole day meandering along and around Front Street and any walks you take will almost inevitably end up back at the thoroughfare. Front Street is at its best on long and languorous summer evenings when the whole of Bermuda seems to be here, though in the quieter months traversing its length is far easier without the crowds.

Government Buildings ***

The grand two-storey colonial edifice on Front Street, the **Cabinet Building** (open Monday–Friday 09:00–17:00), is currently home to Bermuda's senate, who meet weekly to discuss the legislation tabled by the nearby assembly – discuss being the right word as today this is really little more than a debating chamber. Famous names who have walked the corridors of this 19th-century building over the years include Winston Churchill, former President Bush, JFK and Margaret Thatcher. British Prime Minister Churchill and American President Dwight Eisenhower once held a crucial wartime conference at the grand wooden table that still resides in the building today, though bizarrely the meeting actually took place outside Bermuda.

Like the parliament in London, you can visit, as public access was guaranteed when it first opened, and there is also a 'black rod' (an ebony staff topped with a golden lion, fashioned by the Crown Jewellers in London) on display, which is carried by a police officer every year as part of the ceremony to mark the opening of parliament. In front of the limestone building is Bermuda's **Cenotaph**, erected in 1920 and now commemorating the Bermudians who fell in both world wars. If it looks familiar to British visitors, it should: it was modelled on its counterpart at Whitehall in London.

Above: *The neo-Classical Sessions House whose watchtower was added to honour the Golden Jubilee of Queen Victoria.*

Just across the road from the Cabinet Building is the old **Town Hall**, a squat and relatively unspectacular building. When the parliament first moved to Hamilton from St George the assembly sat here before moving up the hill to the voluminous **Sessions House**. Bermuda not only has the honour of having one of the oldest parliaments in the world outside England, but surely also one of the most well travelled.

Head up the dauntingly grand wooden staircase (look out as you go for the statues that are said to have been shipped in from the Houses of Parliament in London) and you can take in a session of the very British-style parliament complete with its wig-clad speaker and mace-armed Sergeant-at-Arms. The gatherings here are quite a formal affair and you won't get in if you show up sporting your beach gear.

On the exterior you cannot miss the huge **Clock Tower** and its enormous clock – with a suitably large 45kg (100lb) pendulum. The terracotta colonnades, which were added to mark Queen Victoria's Golden Jubilee in 1887, are also striking. If you spot any lavishly clad judges coming or going they will likely be from the **Supreme Court** that occupies the lower floor of Sessions House. Interestingly, the Supreme Court can operate with a minimum of three appointed justices and a maximum

THE BIGGEST SLICE OF EMPIRE

When Hong Kong slipped out of the British Empire as the royal yacht *Britannia* carried Prince Charles out of Victoria Harbour in 1997 Bermuda was left as the most populous British Overseas Territory. It stands tall in what is still the world's largest empire (on which the sun still does not ever set), with its 64,000 people dwarfing other 'possessions' such as Pitcairn Island with its four dozen Seventh-Day Adventists, and a flurry of sparsely populated or uninhabitable islands.

of five. At present Bermuda has four Supreme Court judges. The Sessions House is home to another legal body, the Court of Appeal.

Churches of Church Street ★★

The most famous church in Hamilton is the Anglican **Cathedral of the Most Holy Trinity**. This neo-Gothic edifice stands proudly on Church Street sporting a very European appearance, all vaulted arches and stained-glass windows. This continues inside where the pulpit and lectern are modelled on St Giles Cathedral in Edinburgh. Mainly built from Bermudian limestone, stone from Scotland and France was also used, together with Indiana oak. When the tower is open it offers good views of Hamilton.

Above: *Wesley Methodist Church owes its existence to Methodist missionaries who travelled to Bermuda from Canada.*

Other churches to look out for are **St Andrew's Presbyterian Church**, which was built in 1846, making it the oldest original church in the city, and **Wesley Methodist Church** (www.wesley.bm). The latter church was founded by Methodists who originally came to Bermuda as missionaries from Nova Scotia.

Although it's not on Church Street, at 13 Cedar Avenue the **Cathedral of St Theresa**, which is at the centre of the Catholic faith on the islands, is also worth seeking out. It is a striking pink structure which, when it was built in the 1920s, was designed to look like a Spanish mission.

BERMUDA'S BACKSIDE

The tourist office might have you believe there is no crime nor any drug problem in Bermuda, but although neither are anywhere near as serious as in North America and Europe, this is not strictly true. The area north of Victoria Street in Hamilton, particularly around Court Street, is known locally as the 'Backside' and this rough-around-the-edges netherworld is best avoided by tourists.

City Hall ★

The striking City Hall is one of Hamilton's most memorable buildings, a grand civic edifice rising behind a phalanx of fountains near the main bus station. Designed by Bermudian architect Wil Onions, it opened to much fanfare in 1960. The ground floor is perhaps not quite as grand as the façade, but it is home to a brooding portrait of Queen Victoria. Upstairs is the

Bermuda National Gallery, moved here in the 1990s, which has a more impressive range of art on display, from the work of European luminaries such as Gainsborough and Rembrandt through to more local talent like the late and much revered Alfred Birdsey, who had his own studio in Bermuda (*see* page 91). The gallery also stages a range of temporary exhibitions, as well as film screenings and an annual modern art competition. Open Monday–Saturday 10:00–16:00, tel: 295-9428, www.ng.bm

Also housed within the expansive City Hall is the **Bermuda Society of Arts Gallery**. The society was started in the 1950s by a group of artists dedicated to encouraging and promoting the visual arts in Bermuda. Today their work takes the form of staging a variety of exhibitions and artistic competitions, with everything from creative local artists to the work of Bermudian photographers and West Indian painters. It is possible to buy some of the works for those looking to purchase a highbrow Bermudian souvenir. Open Monday–Saturday 19:00–16:00, tel: 292-3824, www.bsoa.bm

Perot Post Office ★

One of the most charming build-ings in the city was set up by the eponymous William B Perot who was appointed Postmaster General in 1821. He is renowned not only for opening the post office that still functions on the site today, but also for commis-sioning the lovely park that lies to the rear (*see* page 39) and one of the world's most collectible, not to mention expensive stamps, of which only around a dozen

Below: *St Andrew's Presbyterian Church has been part of life in the City of Hamilton for more than 160 years.*

ROSEDON HOTEL

One of the most elegant and 'Bermudian' places to stay is the Rosedon Hotel on the outskirts of Hamilton. The whitewashed house, with its veranda, lush gardens and distinctive sky blue shutters, reclines away from the modern world. It was built in 1906 by a Mr EJ Thompson and named in honour of his son. The fine woods used to build Rosedon – pine, oak, cherry, redwood and mahogany – were all imported and since the 1950s Rosedon has been open as a guest-house, offering a refined old-world panache, lazy after-noon teas and shady palm-fringed gardens, an oasis where it feels the 21st century is yet to dawn.

Below: *The outdoor pool and lush gardens at the Rosedon Hotel.*

are thought still to be in existence. This is the place from which to send your postcards. The façade of Perot Post Office is striking with a stark white sheen complemented by jet black windows and shuttered doors; the interior has a less impressive, more modern feel.

Perot himself lived next to the post office in Par-la-Ville House. This old building is now the home of the Bermuda Library and the Bermuda Historical Society Museum and worth visiting. After passing the portrait of Sir George Somers as you enter, seek out the library on the ground floor (the lending library is upstairs). The **Bermuda Library** was founded in 1839 and has perhaps the finest collection of books about Bermuda and by Bermudian authors anywhere. You are as welcome here reading today's copy of the *Royal Gazette* or recent editions of international newspapers and magazines as you are seeking out copies of newspapers from over a century ago.

The **Bermuda Historical Society Museum,** meanwhile, is a wonderful period piece with a collection of fine china and Bermuda cedar, as well as the pine floors Perot shipped in from America. Exhibits include a letter to Bermuda from George Washington petitioning the locals for help in the fight against the South during the American Civil War, a 17th-century cedar table, and a model of the ill-fated *Sea Venture*, as well as the twin ships Somers built to continue the journey to Virginia; other Somers artefacts include his old sea chest and com-pass. Look out also for an old 'Hog Penny' shilling, once a fond part of the islands' cur-rency that is commemorated by a pub of the same name in the city. Other exhibits include portraits of Sir George Somers and his wife Lady Somers, and an exhibit detail-ing the detention of thou-sands of South African Boers

on the islands at the beginning of the 20th century. The British sent the prisoners from the Boer Wars to Bermuda, as the islands were so far away that there was no chance that the captives would be able to escape and make the journey home. The museum is also home to an ornate sedan chair, which is believed to have come from England where it was constructed in the latter half of the 18th century. Today the 'throne' has been restored to its full glory, and offers museum visitors the rare chance to see this type of structure, as it is thought to be the only surviving sedan chair in the western hemisphere.

Above: *The gleaming white City Hall with its clock tower and myriad fountains is one of the City of Hamilton's most impressive buildings.*

Parks **

Barr's Bay Park lies at the north end of Front Street, by the Bermuda Yacht Club. From here you can watch the ferries bustling around and, at weekends, junior sailors learning the ropes in the protected waters. **Par-la-Ville,** meanwhile, was laid out behind Perot Post Office in the 1800s. Its pathways spread around the flower-bedecked hillside, with benches on hand to make it an ideal venue for a picnic. One famous visitor, the American writer Mark Twain, was said to have been disappointed that the park's large rubber tree was not bearing a harvest of hot water bottles and rubber shoes. Today's lunching office workers and resting tourists, however, seem perfectly happy with the fact that it isn't.

Victoria Park stretches off behind City Hall and is worth visiting in summer for its regular free lunchtime musical performances, and in the run-up to Christmas when it is the setting for festive concerts. Watch out for shady characters at night, though. The ornate bandstand here was built to mark Queen Victoria's Golden Jubilee in 1887.

TWAIN'S GREAT LOVE

Legendary American writer and traveller Mark Twain was much enamoured with Bermuda. Countering claims that its small size meant that there was little here to detain travellers for any great time he said that 'Bermuda is the biggest small place in the world'. His most famous eulogy, 'You die and go to heaven. I'd rather stay in Bermuda', is a perennial favourite of tourist office copywriters.

City of Hamilton at a Glance

BEST TIMES TO VISIT

From Apr through to Oct the City of Hamilton's outdoor spaces buzz with life, but the humidity can make the city stifling between Jun and Aug. From Nov to Mar Bermuda's Heart & Soul programme brings free activities in the form of guided tours (Mon), performances by the Bermuda Islands Pipe Band (Mon), Gombey dancing (Tue) and cookery demonstrations (Wed) to the capital. Pick up a leaflet from the Visitor Services Bureau on Front Street for more information.

GETTING THERE

All but one of Bermuda's bus routes start or finish in Hamilton, making the capital easily accessible from almost anywhere on the island. Those travelling to/from St David's Island will need to change buses at the airport. Ferries from Sandys, Southampton, Paget and Warwick run to Hamilton. From early May until mid-Nov there is also a ferry service between St George and Hamilton.

GETTING AROUND

The city is easily navigable on foot. There are also a couple of cycle companies offering moped and scooter hire, as well as an abundant supply of taxis. During the cruise ship season (Apr–Oct) you can also travel around the capital on a horse-drawn cart.

WHERE TO STAY

LUXURY

Fairmont Hamilton Princess, 76 Pitt's Bay Road, tel: 295-3000, fax: 295-1914, www.fairmont.com One of Bermuda's oldest and most historic hotels enjoys a hard-to-beat location on the edge of the city, with many rooms boasting stunning harbour views. The hotel has almost everything you need, from high-class shops and a day spa to three swimming pools and a choice of dining options. Guests can also take advantage of the ferry transfer to its sister hotel, the Fairmount Southampton (see page 108) where a private beach awaits.
Waterloo House, 100 Pitt's Bay Road, tel: 295-4480, fax: 295-2585, www.waterloohouse.com This small Relais & Chateaux hotel reclines on the waterfront just west of the city centre. An old-world ambience pervades the property, whose guest rooms are elegant. If you really want to push the boat out then book a suite with a private Jacuzzi.

MID-RANGE

Rosedon, 61 Pitt's Bay Road, tel: 295-1640, fax: 295-5904, www.rosedonbermuda.com This wonderfully traditional Bermudian house and its more modern annex have 47 charming rooms. The size, class and price of the rooms varies considerably, with rates

of the most affordable double rooms falling into the budget category. However, it is really worth spending the extra on the superior rooms or checking out the seven-day packages. Rosedon also has its own palm-fringed swimming pool and one of the friendliest cats in Bermuda. (See panel, page 38).
Royal Palms Hotel & Restaurant, tel: 292-1854, fax: 292-1946, www.royalpalms.bm This small hotel is renowned locally for its typical Bermudian décor, lush gardens and the Ascot restaurant. Rooms are large, comfortable and individually furnished.

BUDGET

Oxford House, 20 Woodbourne Avenue, tel: 295-0503, fax: 295-0250, www.oxfordhouse.bm This typical Bermudian-style town house has 12 graceful guest rooms that can accommodate up to four people.
Edgehill Manor, 36 Rosemont Avenue, tel: 295-7124, fax: 295-3850, www.bermuda.com/edgehill Colonial-style mansion with nine spacious rooms, all with private balconies. There is also a private garden and an outdoor pool.
Bay City Guest House, 53 Pitt's Bay Road, tel: 295-1275, fax: 295-3166. The vibrant blue exterior makes this pleasant 12-room inn hard to miss.

City of Hamilton at a Glance

Rosemont Guest Apartments, 41 Rosemont Avenue, tel: 292-1055, fax: 292-1055, www.rosemont.bm Stay in a spacious room, studio apartment or opulent suite.

WHERE TO EAT

LUXURY
Barracuda, 5 Burnaby Hill, tel: 292-1609. One of the few restaurants in Bermuda with a chic, modern European feel, the Barracuda serves up first-rate fish in intimate surroundings. The fresh oysters, spiny lobster and seafood pasta are hard to fault.
Port O' Call, 87 Front Street, tel: 295-5373. Featured in every Bermudian's list of the islands' best restaurants, the Port O' Call is an intimate eatery whose menu is dominated by fresh fish and grilled meat.
Harley's (see Fairmont Hamilton Princess). The hotel's signature restaurant serves up excellent cuisine throughout the year. A nightly happy hour and Caribbean Carnival BBQ lend the terrace, with its harbour views, a festive atmosphere from April through to September.
Heritage Court (see Fairmont Hamilton Princess). Shellfish lovers should head here on Thursdays for the Oyster and Chablis evenings.

MID-RANGE
Café Cairo, 93 Front Street, tel: 295-5155. One of the newest restaurants in Bermuda's eating and drinking scene brings a Egyptian boudoir, complete with comfortable sofas and big cushions, to Hamilton's main street. On warmer evenings the ornate outdoor terrace is also a pleasant place to sit. Tangines, delicate fish dishes, daily specials and traditional shisha pipes (water pipes) all go down a treat, and you might just see Michael Douglas, who has been spotted dining here.
L'Oriental, 32 Bermudiana Road, tel: 296-4477. Japanese and Chinese influenced dishes feature on the menu at this relaxed and stylish eatery. In winter the restaurant participates in a dining scheme, which allows you to eat in three of the group's restaurants for a fraction of the cost (see panel, page 25).
Silk, 55 Front Street, tel: 295-0449. This elegant Thai restaurant offers the usual suspects like red, green and yellow curries alongside dishes with a more local slant, like wahoo.

BUDGET
Harbourfront, 21 Front Street, tel: 295-4207. This popular restaurant serving an eclectic menu also has a sushi bar that becomes a budget option during its daily Sushi Happy Hour, which begins at 17:00.
Lemon Tree Café, 7 Queen Street, tel: 292-0235. This small café with a peaceful garden is a favourite of local business people. The huge chicken pie comes highly recommended and sells out quickly.
Pickled Onion, 53 Front Street, tel: 295-2263. Bermuda Fish Sandwiches, hearty tuna melts, tasty nachos and excellent burgers are just some of the filling delights on sale in this British-style pub.

SHOPPING
The majority of shops of interest to visitors are located on Front Street, where you can purchase good value cosmetics and perfume. You will also find a number of jewellers, with Walker Christopher at number nine (tel: 295-1466) well worth visiting.

TOURS AND EXCURSIONS
WildCat Adventure Tours, tel: 293-7433. You can circle Bermuda's main island on a high-speed catamaran. The boat picks up passengers at Flag Pole in Hamilton and also at Penno's Wharf in St George's.

USEFUL CONTACTS
Visitors Service Bureau, Front Street, tel: 295-1480.
Wheels Cycles, 117 Front Street, tel: 292-2245.
Oleander Cycles, 15 Gorham Road, tel: 295-0919.
Smatt's Cycle Livery, 74 Pitts Bay Road, tel: 295-1180.

3
St George's Parish

Named after the man credited with first starting human settlement in Bermuda, Sir George Somers, St George's is the easternmost parish, consisting of the settled islands of St George's itself and St David's, as well as a flurry of smaller islets that are often only accessible by private boat. The beating heart of the parish is St George, easily the most attractive and historical town in Bermuda. Here the centuries peel back, with old whitewashed buildings lacing the narrow streets. The darker side of life from those harsh early colonial days is also clearly on show, with the stocks used for punishment lying all too visibly on the main square.

St George may have lost its capital status to go-getting Hamilton centuries ago, but that simply makes it all the more charming, as it has been able to preserve its glorious architecture without the ravaging demands of modernization. People still live, breathe and work in period buildings in a town where new development is strictly controlled, especially since St George won a coveted place on UNESCO's World Heritage list in 2000. It may get horrendously busy when the cruise ships are in town, but come here at night or out of season and you can really let your imagination run riot.

Nearby St David's Island offers an alternative slice of Bermuda. Here locals seem reluctant to make what they see as the marathon trek to Hamilton and the 'mainland' and hold on dearly to a way of life long lost on the other islands.

DON'T MISS

*** **King's Square:** historical re-enactments in the town's charming main square.
*** **Ordnance Island:** take in the replica of George Somers's ship *Deliverance*.
*** **Churches:** St Peter's, one of Bermuda's oldest buildings.
*** **Museums:** Bermuda's history, heritage and art
*** **Fort St Catherine:** bulwark built to protect against a foreign invasion that never materialized.
*** **Bermuda Biological Station for Research:** gain a better understanding of the islands' diverse marine life.

Opposite: *An old cannon at St David's Battery.*

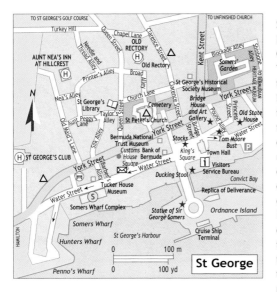

St George

ST GEORGE
King's Square and
Ordnance Island ★★★

The historic heart of the town of St George is on **King's Square**, a waterfront plaza that houses the town hall, the tourist office, the old punishment stocks and a variety of eating and drinking options, as well as the ducking stool where a local 'wench' is regularly ducked for the benefit of tourist cameras. In winter there are also free walking tours and the chance to meet the town mayor on Wednesday and Saturday mornings.

Just offshore, connected by a small bridge, is **Ordnance Island**, which was once used as an ammunition store for the fledgling settlement. The island is now the first landfall of arriving cruise ship passengers, and its other function is to commemorate the man who founded the town, with a striking sculpture of Somers himself (crafted by Desmond Hale Fountain) gesticulating towards town, and a model of one of the ships, the *Deliverance*, which Somers built to continue his storm-ravaged journey to Virginia. You can tour the ship and try to figure out how on earth they packed 150 people into it for their Atlantic voyage. Open daily 09:00–17:00, tel: 297-1459.

Old State House ★★

Reckoned to be the oldest building in Bermuda, this was once the local parliament before the real power moved to Hamilton. It later became the haunt of Scottish Freemasons, and the Masons now pay the princely sum of one peppercorn as their annual rent,

Below: *Model of the Deliverance, one of the ships that Sir George Somers and his crew built after being shipwrecked on the island.*

with the payment subject to a popular public ceremony in April. Prince Charles, a keen architecture buff, was on hand to open the restored State House in 1970 and its façade still boasts a certain severe grandeur best enjoyed as it looms above you when you walk up the lane from King's Square. Note the square roof, quite unusual in Bermuda where the tapered, slanting roofs were normally designed to collect rainwater.

Above: *The Old State House – believed to be the oldest building on the islands.*

Tom Moore Bust *

The bust of Tom Moore looks rather grand for the raffish and scandal-ridden Celtic poet he was said to be. Moore sojourned on Bermuda in 1804 and found time to fall hopelessly in love with the teenage wife of a local moneyed man. His 'Odes to Nea' may not have won any literary prizes, but they add a bit of steamy scandal to respectable St George, and the poet lends his name to one of Bermuda's best restaurants (see page 66).

Somers' Garden **

Verdant Somers' Garden is a lush subtropical park in the centre of St George and has a few well-placed benches where you can sit with the butterflies and watch the world go by, accompanied by the remains (or at least the heart and a few other bits) of Sir George Somers, which are buried here and marked by a memorial. Huge palms stretch skywards across this well-kept oasis, but, as with the rest of the islands, the majority of the vegetation is not indigenous. Open daily 08:00–16:00.

SOMERS' LOST HEART

St George is home to the heart and various other unspecified parts of the man credited with its founding. Sir George Somers is said to have requested that his troublesome ticker be left in his newfound love, Bermuda. His body, though, was pickled in alcohol and shipped back to England where the rest of his remains were returned to his birthplace, Lyme Regis. Today St George is twinned with Lyme Regis and anyone wanting to pay their full respects to Somers has a long journey ahead.

Above: *A squabble among the St George locals ensured that this church, as its name, the Unfinished Church, suggests, was never completed.*

Churches ★★★

Whitewashed **St Peter's Church** reclines just above King's Square and savours its role as one of the oldest Anglican churches in the Western Hemisphere, dating back to 1612. Guided tours tend just to skip around the outside and the graveyard laden with grand headstones – here you will find the grave of **Sir Richard Sharples**, the governor shot dead in 1973 (*see* panel, page 17). It is also well worth delving inside to appreciate the wooden-beamed ceiling with its chandeliers.

The **Unfinished Church,** meanwhile, is an atmospheric ruin that serves as a firm testament to human folly. This grand, Gothic edifice was never completed thanks to a split between members of the congregation (one half left to build their own church) and a siphoning off of funds to repay the damaged cathedral in Hamilton. It has a wonderfully decayed feel and stands brooding, moodily overlooking the trim, neat buildings that comprise the rest of the town.

Museums ★★★

St George's **Historical Society Museum** really succeeds in conjuring up the feel of old Bermuda. Sir George Somers himself seems to approve as his portrait hangs omnipresent over this trim and well-run museum. The rest of this 18th-century building contains four-poster beds, old weapons and solid wooden furnishings. Open 10:00–16:00, tel: 297-0545.

The Tucker House Museum, now owned by the **Bermuda National Trust**, was once the property of one of the most powerful families on the islands, the Tuckers. It is a fine example of an old Bermudian house and dates from around the start of the 18th century. Shipowner Thomas Smith, who also ran a tavern, once lived here, leading then Governor William Popple to turn down a request for it to be used as a court, complaining it was more 'noted for punch than for law'. Tucker family portraits adorn the walls, though not one of perhaps the most famous Tucker, Bermudian leader Henry Tucker; there is, however, one of his brother Thomas Tudor, who became one of the longest serving Treasurers of the United States.

Inside Tucker House Museum the main attraction is the furniture. There are lashings of silver, but it is the Bermudian cedar wood that really stands out. In the drawing room is a cedar tea table from the 18th century thought to have been here since the house was built. Look out also for the Honduran mahogany in the library and the Chippendale tallboy. In the kitchen, spare a thought for **Joseph Hayne Rainey**, a man from South Carolina who progressed from cutting hair in St George to become the first black member of the US House of Representatives. Open

St George's Parish

JOSEPH HAYNE RAINEY 1832–87

The first black congressman to serve in the US House of Representatives, Joseph Hayne Rainey was born into slavery in Georgetown in 1832. When he was around 14 years old Rainey's father purchased his family's freedom and move them to Charleston. Following in his father's footsteps, Rainey became a barber, a trade that he practised in Bermuda between 1862 and 1865 where he lived with his wife before returning to the USA and becoming a congressman in 1870.

daily 10:00–16:00, tel: 297-0545.

The **Old Rectory**, another Bermuda National Trust property, excites with its pirate past – it is said to have been built by a nefarious local character at the tail end of the 19th century. He must have found peace here as legend has it that he later became a man of the cloth. The building's ecclesiastical connection continued with the coming of Alexander Richardson, an English minister, who was given the house as a dowry for marrying a Bermudian woman. Open daily 12:00–17:00 (April–October), and on Wednesdays only from November–March.

The **Bermudian Heritage Museum** is housed in the old haunt of a Masonic lodge that was built in 1843. If you are interested in the black history of Bermuda then this is the place to come as it delves into the stories of the slaves and free black men who have made such an important contribution to Bermudian history. Slavery first came to Bermuda in the 17th century, but emancipation legislation came in 1834, before the USA. This led to some interesting anomalies such as the case of the American slave ship *Enterprise*, which foundered off the islands leading to the freeing of its 73 slave passengers under local law. Many of these slaves settled on Bermuda and their proud descendants still live there today. Open Tuesday–Saturday 10:00–15:00, tel. 297-4126.

AROUND ST GEORGE'S ISLAND
Fort St Catherine ★★★

This is the grandest and most visitor-friendly military installation in the parish – if you only have time to visit one fort this is the one. Enjoying a stunning location overlooking sandy Achilles Bay and St Catherine's Beach, this massive fort boasts a short

Below: *The sturdy hulk of Fort St Catherine – taken from St Catherine's Beach.*

Left: *A cannon protruding through the ramparts at Alexandra Battery.*

audiovisual show and museum exhibits to back up the drama of its monstrously proportioned guns. The guns themselves point out to sea, but have never been fired in anger. Peer below the guns and you can see the spot where Somers and his straggling group of survivors first staggered ashore following their fateful shipwreck.

Fort Albert and Fort Victoria ★

These long-forgotten forts lie increasingly overgrown near the similarly dilapidated and abandoned Club Med. Those with time at St Catherine's may want to scramble up the slope to see these once mighty bastions that nature is slowly reclaiming. They are seldom open these days and the time when they could fire shells weighing over 227kg (500lb) is long gone.

Alexandra Battery ★★

One of the unique features of this battery are the metal flash plates, 'Gibraltar Shields', that were built around the cannon to protect the artillery gunners from incoming fire. Just below the battery is the small

---

SHOTS IN ANGER

At one point heavily militarized Bermuda boasted well over 50 forts and gun batteries. The British were paranoid about the defence of Bermuda and went to epic lengths to ensure its safety, leaving a legacy of fortifications dotted all over the islands. In the end only one fort ever fired in anger (practising was also often ruled out – by the 20th century the big guns, if fired, would have smashed windows for miles around). Two shots were fired in 1614 when the Spanish approached. Luckily they acted as a deterrent (as the garrison only had one more shell left) and the Spanish hastily made off.

Above: *Located in a sheltered cove, Tobacco Bay is a popular spot with snorkellers.*

beach where the *Deliverance* was built and launched, as Somers's shipwrecked survivors sought to eventually complete their journey to Virginia.

Gates Fort Park ★★

This modest little battery is a great spot to watch the powerful tugs sweeping in and out of St George's harbour through the dangerously narrow Town Cut. Plans have been mooted to blast away at the rocks and widen the Cut to allow in cruise ships, but thankfully nothing has thus far been agreed. There are a few guns here, and the rocks in front of the battery are a pleasant spot to idle away an hour or so staring out at the ocean or enjoying a picnic.

St George's Beaches ★★

St George's Parish boasts some decent stretches of sand, which can often be a bit quieter than the beaches further south, especially if there is no cruise ship in town. **Tobacco Bay** is perhaps the most famous – a glorious little sweep of puffy white sand with rocks offshore for snorkelling and a modest café that is open in summer. **St Catherine's Beach** enjoys

---

SHAKESPEARE AND BERMUDA

Although the famous bard never actually ventured out to Bermuda it is widely thought to have been the inspiration behind his last play, and some say his most autobiographical, with Prospero as Shakespeare relinquishing his fading powers, in *The Tempest*. The play, like the settlement of Bermuda, starts with a massive storm and shipwreck on a remote island.

an unparalleled setting, with the hulk of Fort St Catherine dominating one flank. **Achilles Bay,** meanwhile, is the quietest of the three – another public beach that offers good swimming.

FERRY POINT AND FERRY POINT ISLAND

The closest most visitors to Bermuda get to **Ferry Point** is asking the taxi driver what the strange-looking tower is in the distance as they head to or from the airport across the causeway. Those taking time to walk or cycle down here to explore this forgotten slice of Bermuda, where the railway used to run, are amply rewarded.

Martello Tower *

This sturdy rounded Martello tower, built in 1823, is an unmistakable sight and you can get into it across the drawbridge that vaults its moat as you descend on the Railway Trail towards Ferry Point. To the northeast look out for Whalebone Bay where an old magazine watches over a forgotten beach.

Burnt Point Fort **

Past the Martello tower you can make out the remains of a fort nearby and then another scramble of ruins out on the point itself, which is also known as Burnt Point. There is not much to see here after you pick your way over the volcanic rocks, but it is an atmospheric spot to stand and try to conjure up a time when soldiers used to watch over the ferries that once ran across to Coney Island from this spot. Look out towards Smith's Parish and you can make out the supports that used to house an old railway that is now just a rapidly fading memory.

Below: *The Martello tower at Ferry Point.*

THE MOST PRECIOUS RESOURCE

Although it is surrounded by water on all sides Bermuda is not blessed with any rivers or streams. Water has been a precious resource since the days when the first settlers arrived, with roofs designed to trickle down rainfall and collect it. You can still see this type of roof all around the island today.

Bermuda Biological Station for Research ★★★

This station is a lot more fun than its name suggests. Since its foundation over a century ago, it has been conducting its own research and welcoming students from all over the world who have flocked to investigate the fascinating local marine system and the nearby deep Atlantic. Their work includes research into environmental impact, and they run free tours on a Wednesday that illuminate their work. In the past they have also run trips, including some out to legendary Nonsuch Island (*see* page 65). You can also check out their 35m (115ft) *Weatherbird II* research vessel. Tel: 297-1880, www.bbsr.edu

St David's Island

This island was dominated for decades by the US military, and since they left in 1995 it has slipped back into its lotus-eating lifestyle: here Hamilton seems a long

way away. Despite the presence of Bermuda's airport, this is a relaxing spot strewn with beaches and quiet residential communities, and it is steeped in military history. The islanders, still renowned as they have been for centuries as accomplished fishermen, harbour a palpable sense of distinctive identity.

St David's Lighthouse was built in 1879 and it casts a striking presence with its gleaming white tower capped with a bright red band. You can climb to the top and take in a sweeping view of Bermuda – if the door is locked just ask at the kiosk next door.

Nearby is **St David's Battery**, which is part of **Great Head Park**. Here you can amble around the cliff-top fortifications and take a good look at the looming guns, positioned here at the start of the 20th century, which still guard the approaches to St George. Look out also

Left: *The sea laps the shore at the tranquil Gunner's Bay Park.*
Opposite: *Feast your eyes on the dramatic views from the top of St David's lighthouse on the eponymous island. This red and white beacon has been safeguarding sailors since 1879.*

for the impressive new boat-shaped memorial erected to commemorate the souls who have lost their lives at sea, which was unveiled by Prince Andrew (Duke of York) in 2005.

Gunner's Bay Park is a smaller park that sits right on the water looking back towards St George's and some of the smaller islands. A historic building worth checking out in the vicinity of the airport is **Carter House** (open Tuesday, Wednesday, Thursday and Saturday 10:00–16:00, tel: 293-5960), thought to be the oldest building on St David's at around 300 years. The museum sheds light on St David's history, playing a crucial role in keeping the unique spirit of the island intact. The gardens are also an enjoyable place to wander around on a sunny day.

When the US base and airport were built, landfill connected **Cooper's Island** to St David's, which means today you can easily get onto this 'island'. Here you will find the sandy beaches at **Clearwater**, where there is a beach house and playground, and **Turtle Bay,** as well as the **Cooper's Island Nature Reserve**, with its ramble of walking trails.

AT THE FOREFRONT OF RESEARCH

Pioneers in the field of ocean health, the Bermuda Biological Station for Research opened the first International Centre for Ocean and Human Health. Its remit is to study factors that upset the ecological balance of the ocean, such as pollution, and to monitor the use of marine substances in the field of human health (e.g. pharmaceuticals and nutritional supplements). The country's territorial waters are also considered ideal for predicting or warning against ecological change in developing countries with tropical coastlines.

St George's Parish at a Glance

Weatherwise St George's is a pleasant place to visit at any time. The island's oldest settlement of St George is at its liveliest between April and October, when a steady stream of cruise ship passengers descend upon the town. Free guided walks, a chance to meet the mayor, and re-enactments of historical events like the 'ducking stool' help keep the town alive on Wednesdays and Saturdays during the winter. There is also a visitor golf tournament at St George's Golf Course on Wednesdays between November and March.

The most pleasant way to arrive in St George is on the ferry from Hamilton (journey time 60–90 minutes), which operates between early May and early November. Buses from Hamilton (routes 1, 3, 10 and 11) also operate a regular service to and from St George via the airport.

The best way to get around the town of St George is on foot; however, anyone who really wants to explore the parish should consider renting a moped or a bicycle. Taxis, which can be hired by the hour for tours (the minimum rental period is three hours), provide an alternative and a safer way of getting around. St George's Mini-Bus Service (tel: 297-8199), which picks up passengers in King's Square, provides a more affordable way of travelling around the parish; however, these can be busy and do not always take the most direct route. There is a taxi rank in the main square, King's Square, for point-to-point journeys.

LUXURY

The St George's Club, Rose Hill Street, tel: 297-1200, fax: 297-8003, www.st georgeclub.com Combining traditional hotel accommodation and timeshare units, this club is a collection of one-and two-bedroom apartments situated around three freshwater swimming pools. Sitting atop Rose Hill, the club affords good views over St George. The winning ingredients for family groups are fully equipped kitchens, two on site restaurants, laundry facilities and a shop.

BUDGET

Aunt Nea's Inn at Hillcrest, 1 Nea's Alley, tel: 297-1630, fax: 297-1908, www.aunt neas.com This traditional Bermudian guesthouse nestles on the hillside overlooking the town of St George. Wrought-iron or four-poster beds heighten the luxurious feel that pervades this elegant home.

Old Rectory, 1 Broad Alley, tel: 297-4261. If you want to stay in this attractive white-washed historic building at the heart of St George then book well in advance, as there are only two guest rooms. It is also possible to rent the whole cottage.

MID-RANGE

Café Gio, 36 Water Street, tel: 297-1307. A range of daily specials and the ubiquitous Bermuda seafood chowder accompany a range of pizzas, pastas, sandwiches and salads. The food at this Italian-styled eatery is simple but delicious, and the waterside terrace is a real winner.

White Horse Pub and Restaurant, 8 King's Square, tel: 297-1838. A prime harbour-front location, hearty dishes and fish specials ensure that this St George pub-restaurant is always busy.

Freddie's Pub and Restaurant, 3 King's Square, tel: 297-1717. Grab a snack at the sports bar or head upstairs to the more formal dining area, from where you can watch the hustle and bustle of St George life.

Tavern By The Sea, 14 Water Street, tel: 297-3305. The waterfront tavern's terrace is a great place for a light lunch or quiet drink.

St George's Parish at a Glance

Black Horse Tavern, 101 St David's Road, St David's Island, tel: 297-1991. Bermudians wax lyrical about the seafood served at this restaurant, claiming that it is the best on the islands. People certainly seem to travel from all over Bermuda to dine here.

BUDGET

Dennis's Hideaway, St David's Island, tel: 297-0044. Dennis Lamb served fish chowder, scallops, conch and mussel pie here from 1967 until he passed away a few years ago. Today his son Grahame (nicknamed Sea-Egg) is at the helm of this eccentric and somewhat dilapidated eatery, which feels about a million miles away from the polished restaurants that cover the rest of the islands. You are welcome to take your own alcohol when you come here for a meal, with many locals claiming that drinking is a necessity. It is unwise to turn up on spec as the restaurant is often closed.

Cyber Café Latte, Water Street, tel: 297-8196. This is a great place in St George to surf the web and to exchange second-hand books. This café also serves a range of sandwiches and snacks, which you can either take away or enjoy from a comfortable sofa.

SHOPPING

Book Cellar, 5 Water Street, tel: 297-0448. This compact bookstore is a great place to pick up books about Bermuda.

Dockside Glass, 3 Bridge Street, tel: 297-3908. This small boutique stocks brightly coloured glassware including delicate fish, vases and plates, as well as delicious Bermuda Rum Cake in 11 flavours.

Somers Wharf, Waterside retailers selling a selection of refined clothing and classy souvenirs.

Davidson's, Water Street. Sells Bermuda T-shirts, ties, tea towels and straw hats.

Paradise Gift Shop, King's Square, tel: 297-1732. Another great place to pick up bright and gaudy T-shirts as well as other Bermuda-themed souvenirs.

Robertson's Drugstore, 24 York Street, tel: 297-1828. The pharmacy has been curing the ills of the town for over seven decades, but this is more than a drugstore, selling everything from postcards and beach accessories to Cuban cigars.

Vera P Card, 7 Water Street. Delicate ceramic figurines, watches and jewellery are on sale, while plates with Bermudian scenes make more unusual gifts and souvenirs.

Carole Holding Print & Craft Shop, King's Square, tel: 297-1833. Carole cites the ocean view from her home as well as the island's attractive natural landscapes as the inspiration for her watercolours, which have found their way onto a range of gifts including mugs, table mats and chopping boards. You can also buy Carole's products at the Fairmont Southampton and from her shop in Front Street, City of Hamilton.

Crissons, Water Street and York Street. This upscale jeweller has two branches in the historic town of St George.

TOURS AND EXCURSIONS

Coral Sea Cruises, tel: 236-3207. Take a glass-bottomed boat tour from St George harbour.

USEFUL CONTACTS

Visitors Service Bureau, King's Square, tel: 297-1642.
Eve's Cycles, 1 Water Street, tel: 236-0839. Centrally located place to hire cycles and mopeds.
Oleander Cycles, 26 York Street, tel: 297-0478.
KS Water Sports, Waterfront by the White Horse Pub and Restaurant, tel: 297-4155. Offering jet-ski hire.
St George's Parasail Water Sports, Somers Wharf, tel: 297-1542.
St George's Golf Club, 1 Park Road, tel: 297-8067.

4
Hamilton Parish

Hamilton is often the source of much confusion for visitors, as, despite its name, the parish does not actually house the eponymous capital city, which is located 13km (8 miles) to the west. Instead it takes its name from the Scottish peer James Hamilton, the second Marquis of Hamilton. One of the major adventurers in the Bermuda Company, Hamilton gave his name to the islands' second most eastern parish back in 1615, which was known then as Hamilton Tribe. Things didn't pan out quite as the entrepreneur had planned, however, and he died of malignant fever just ten years later at the age of 36. Some Bermudians say that even in death the Marquis did not find peace, as his son was executed for treason almost a quarter of a century later in 1649.

Its chief investor may have been unlucky, but this attractive corner of Bermuda has plenty to offer tourist visitors, despite a relative lack of hotels.

Its sinewy shape houses two of Bermuda's most popular tourist attractions in the sublime **Crystal and Fantasy Caves** and the illuminating **Bermuda Aquarium** complex (which also includes the **National History Museum** and **Bermuda Zoo**). Those who venture away from the main tourist sights are rewarded with a sprinkling of quieter corners in which to relax away from the crowds, including the limestone caves that punctuate the north shore and are at their most accessible from the grounds of the **Grotto Bay Hotel** and **Blue Hole Park**. In addition, the parish boasts the islands'

ATLANTIC OCEAN — ST GEORGE • St George's — Hamilton — Sandys — Pembroke HAMILTON • — Smith's — Devonshire — Paget — Warwick — Southampton

---

DON'T MISS

*** **Crystal and Fantasy Caves:** impressive stalactites and stalagmites formed over millions of years.
*** **Blue Hole Park and Walsingham Nature Reserve:** peace and tranquillity just metres from the main road.
*** **The Swizzle Inn:** pop in for a legendary rum swizzle.
*** **Bermuda Aquarium, Museum and Zoo:** learn about Bermuda's natural history and its marine life.
*** **Bermuda Railway Museum and Trail:** a must for rail enthusiasts.

Opposite: *Harrington Sound is Bermuda's inland lake.*

Above: *Dramatic stalactite formations await visitors to the Crystal Caves.*

most exclusive real estate at **Tucker's Point**, where the world's rich and famous have chosen to house their Bermudian hideaways. Hamilton Parish is also popular with trainspotters, who come to check out the **Railway Museum**, and with partygoers who flock here to enjoy a potent Bermuda Rum Swizzle at the legendary **Swizzle Inn**.

BAILEY'S BAY
Crystal and Fantasy Caves ★★★

This subterranean wonderland was only discovered as recently as 1907 when two boys chased a wayward cricket ball and chanced upon an entrance into the cave complex. They let down a rope into the cave, but had to scramble back up without finding the ball. Their impromptu visit was, however, soon followed up by more seasoned cave explorers. Over the years it has been fully developed, but it has still not lost the magical aura that enthralled countless visitors, including Mark Twain.

Today visitors are led by a torch-wielding guide down into the stalactite and stalagmite-encrusted netherworld on guided tours that last around 20 minutes – note the sign as you enter, threatening fines and even imprisonment for damaging the interior – it is deadly serious. Note also that it is a fairly steep descent, which means a heart-pumping scramble back up that may be too much for some visitors.

The highlight of the **Crystal Caves** is the 15m (55ft) deep, cobalt blue lake that reflects the weird and wonderful formations all around; some say that they can see images as eclectic as a dragon, a figure of Christ, a sitting Buddha or even the Manhattan skyline. Try to walk just behind the guide before the whole group descends onto the pontoons and shatters the mirror-effect with ripples.

The **Fantasy Cave** is a more recently opened sibling, which first welcomed visitors in 2001. It may not be as impressive, but the combined ticket option makes it reasonable value. Inside, more stalactites and stalagmites await as you descend 37m (120ft) below Bermuda's surface. Look out for the shadowy passageways that lead off into territories only explored by intrepid cave divers, who can follow them all the way out to the ocean. Open daily 09:00–17:00, tel: 293-0640, http://caves.bm

Blue Hole Park and Walsingham Nature Reserve ★★★

This sleepy little tract of parkland is that rare thing in Bermuda – a local secret. Everyone has a different name for it and a different idea of where various parts start and end, but this need not trouble visitors once you have found it. Few arrivals rushing across the nearby causeway from the airport even know the parkland lies just to the south of the road, but there is a small car park for mopeds and the bus also stops nearby at the Grotto Bay Resort.

The main trail scoops south along the coastline, opening up into lovely little coves, mangrove swamps, sunken caves swimming with brightly coloured fish,

PINK AND PROUD

Bermuda's famously pink sands come from myriad pieces of broken coral and calcium carbonate from other marine invertebrates which have been ground down by the elements. The pinkest pieces are particles from tiny single-shelled animals called foraminifera, with the strength of colour dependent on how fine the particles are. With little sediment in these clear ocean waters the effect is even more pronounced especially at sunrise or sunset.

Below: *Hamilton Parish's best kept secret: the coves, sunken caves, bright fish and grotto of Blue Hole Park.*

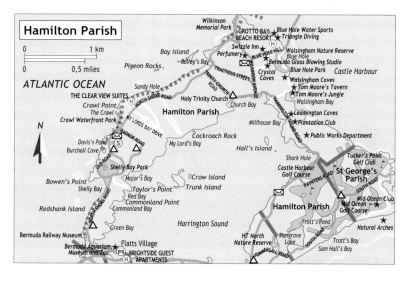

and its own blue grotto. The rocks in this part of Bermuda are particularly old, with some said to date back as far as 800,000 years ago, when the islands were still being formed.

It is hard to believe that this tranquil area used to house a rubbish tip until relatively recently. Today it makes a great getaway where it feels as if modern Bermuda is very far away indeed. Follow the trail all the way south and it comes out at the famous Tom Moore's Tavern restaurant, which sadly does not offer lunch (although it may open on request, tel: 293-8020). From here you can circle back around to the Crystal Caves or retrace your steps to the causeway.

The Swizzle Inn ★★★

A real Bermudian institution, this old inn is home to the famous **Bermuda Rum Swizzle**, whose potency has led to the inn's motto of 'Swizzle Inn, Stagger Out'. If you are feeling cheesy, have your photo taken at the board outside; before heading in, making sure you heed the sign warning that graffiti is banned on the exterior of the inn. Inside, graffiti is actually actively encouraged, with

---

MORE THAN A BUSINESS CARD

Be careful when flashing your business card in Bermuda. Until the early 20th century 'calling cards' amongst the upper classes indicated that an individual had enough wealth not to have to work for a living. As middle classes emerged things changed and they metamorphosed into the modern business card. It still might be wise to avoid business cards on a first dinner meeting in case you end up having to settle the bill.

an orgy of scrawled messages covering every inch, accompanying the army of business cards that are stuck to the walls.

The portions are huge, with a plate of nachos easily enough to feed a nuclear family in other parts of the world, but it is the drinks that most people come for, especially that famous, or rather notorious, Bermuda Rum Swizzle. This tart and refreshing rum concoction is served up in various sizes here, but as it packs quite a punch make sure not to order too much, especially if you are travelling by moped.

Flatts Village
Bermuda Aquarium, Museum and Zoo ★★★

Opened back in 1926 this is one of the island's must-see attractions, enjoyable no matter the weather. Although some of the enclosures and tanks are too small – which justifiably rankles some visitors – this is an interesting half-day trip for people of all ages.

The first section that you encounter is the **Aquarium** whose scattering of smaller tanks house an octopus and scores of other marine species. The main focus is on the **North Rock**, a 260,000-litre (140,000-gallon) coral reef that teems with myriad marine life, from shimmering shoals of small fish through to chunky grouper, fierce-looking barracuda and shadowy nurse sharks. There is a bench surrounded by a mirror where you can take it all in; it is great for kids, who can sit here for ages watching the parade.

Connecting the aquarium to the **Natural History Museum** is a smallish seal pool where a quartet of seals eagerly await their daily public feedings. There are a number of touch screens and audiovisual displays to entertain kids and big kids alike, including an informative four-minute film that sheds light on the formation of the islands.

Wreck and Reef Diving

Bermuda's shallow and warm waters are a haven for divers, with more than 300 wrecks and around 520km^2 (200 sq miles) of easily accessible reef. With an average depth of just 14–15m (45–50ft) the islands are a good place for beginners to learn to dive, with PADI certified courses available from reputable operators like Blue Water Divers and Watersports (www.divebermuda.com).

Below: *One of many species of tropical fish at the Bermuda Aquarium.*
Bottom: *Flamingo enclosure in the Bermuda Zoo.*

Look out also for information on one of Bermuda's eco-success stories, **Nonsuch Island** (*see* page 65).

RATTLE AND SHAKE

In retrospect Bermuda's railway should have been a non-starter: a massively expensive scheme involving cutting through solid rock and 33 vaulting bridges, all to serve the islands' tiny population. The 32km (21-mile) line opened in 1931 but by the time US troops arrived with their automobiles in World War II it was clear the train's days on Bermuda were numbered. The line closed in 1946 and the whole set-up was sold and shipped off to British Guiana. You can still follow sections of the Railway Trail and pay a visit to the modest Railway Museum.

Past the café that lies outside the museum is the modest zoo with its trail that loops around a well-stocked flamingo enclosure and into the **Islands of the Caribbean**, where you can walk amongst the Brazilian acouchi, scarlet ibis, the terrapins and the golden lion tamarin. Right on **Harrington Sound** are a couple of viewing platforms where you can admire the views and if you are lucky spy a spotted eagle ray hurling itself out of the water. Other zoological attractions include **Islands of Australasia**, the **Galapagos Tortoises** and a **South American Aviary**. Open daily 09:00–17:00, tel: 293-2727, www.bamz.org

Bermuda Railway Museum and Trail ★★★

This tiny little museum, run by the enthusiastic and colourful Rosa Hollis, is a quirky little place that is pleasingly incongruous in slick, modern-day Bermuda. It is an apt testament to the weird little railway that cost so much to build, but which ultimately proved as preposterous and unworkable as many locals had continued to insist during its stunningly expensive construction. The museum is housed in the old Aquarium Station building, which used to perform a joint function as a waiting room and a goods shed.

Below: *Black-and-white photographs on display at the Railway Museum bring Bermuda's ill-fated railway back to life.*

Opening hours at the museum are irregular; just pull up and look out for Rosa. There is no entry fee as such but donations are welcome as she still has to pay rent on the site. The actual museum is awash with old maps, train models and signage, with a short taped audio commentary serving as a wonderfully old-fashioned introduction (it is quite a surreal experience to listen

to Rosa's recorded voice recounting the railway's history while she is standing in the museum with you).

From the museum you can strike out along the **Railway Trail** itself. You can head either east towards **Shelly Bay Park** and further on to **Bailey's Bay**, or a short distance west to the **Flatts Inlet**, where the famously high railway bridge once stood (air force pilots used to test their skills, and the nerves of the locals, by flying right under it). You will have to cut south across the Flatts road bridge if you want to follow the Railway Trail down into Smith's Parish proper.

Shelley Bay Park ★
On the North Shore near Flatts, this modest coastal park with its pink beaches and ocean views is a popular place on a sunny day. It is something of a family favourite thanks to its usually calm seas and the shallow waters that allow safe paddling, swimming and snorkelling. There are also changing facilities, a children's playground, and a beach house that rents out snorkelling gear and towels in summer. In winter things tend to be a lot quieter.

Above: *The prime real estate and luxury yachts of Tucker's Town.*

A Word of Caution

If you're travelling around Bermuda by moped or scooter some local riders say it is wise to ride in the middle of the lane to prevent car drivers from attempting rash over-taking manoeuvres. A helmet must also be worn at all times. Moped accidents do happen and sadly they are sometimes fatal. The causeway linking Hamilton and St George's is particularly dangerous, so if you are not familiar with this type of vehicle, are not used to driving on the left, or are in any way unsure about your ability then it is safer to travel by bus or taxi.

Above: *The exclusive Tucker's Point Golf Club.*

TUCKER'S TOWN

The most exclusive real estate in Bermuda lies within Tucker's Town (named after governor Daniel Tucker who envisaged that the area could become the island's new capital in the 17th century), though often locals cannot agree whether Tucker's Town itself lies in St George's, Smith's or Hamilton Parish. The truth is that its fuzzy-edged environs probably cross into all three, though here, for the sake of clarity, it is being neatly popped into Hamilton Parish. What is certain is that this is a multimillionaire's paradise despite its rather dubious founding, when much of the land was snatched from the local black population. Such high rollers as American presidential candidate Ross Perot, mayor of New York City Michael Bloomberg and Italian premier and media mogul Silvio Berlusconi all enjoy prime cuts of ultra-exclusive Tucker's Town real estate, as do many less renowned but equally important captains of industry and finance. Some residences hide behind high walls and burly security guards, though there is nothing to stop you taking a moped around the winding streets of this prettily neat part of Bermuda, which often feels more like the staged TV world of *The Truman Show* than a real, living place.

Cheeky taxi drivers can fill you in on who lives where on a guided tour and may also sneak you up for a glimpse of the exclusive Tucker's Point Golf Club and private Tucker's Point Beach Club. Massive changes are currently afoot at Tucker's Point, with ambitious general manager Mark Orchard at the helm. The spectacular 5816m (6361yd) hillside course was joined by a spanking new 1800m² (20,000 sq ft) clubhouse in 2005 (the sublime food has already won awards), and a deluxe hotel is slated to open by 2008 on the site of the old Castle Harbour Hotel.

If you don't want to stump up the $85,000 joining fee, concierges at the island's better hotels can usually snare you a round or two off peak, though don't try to use locker 67 as this is said to be Nick Faldo's favourite – it is the score he shot to win the US Masters. The 19th hole at Tucker's Point is one of the most enjoyable, with the chance to share a drink perhaps with the likes of the aforementioned Nick Faldo or Michael Douglas at the elegant hardwood bar. For those looking to stay longer there are multi-million dollar homes for sale with views to match and the 'fractional ownership' Residence Club, which offers a relatively affordable slice of la dolce vita. www.tuckerspoint.com

NONSUCH ISLAND

As well as having a wonderful name this small island, which officially lies within St George's Parish (but which you get to by boat from Tucker's Town), is one of Bermuda's finest examples of environmental preservation. Here the once thriving cahow bird, only found on Bermuda, has been saved from extinction, with a flourishing population that some estimates say will rise to 1000 pairs on the island by 2020. Hurricane Fabian caused extensive damage to Nonsuch in 2003, but the dedicated local environmentalists who have made such progress over the years are determined to keep the project running and carefully manage the number of visitors allowed on supervised tours. Check with the tourist office for current details of trips.

CAHOW

Experts believe that the *Ptedorma cahow*, or the Bermuda petrel, has been present on the islands for more than 300,000 years. This bird, which was once so prevalent, has gained a special place in the hearts of Bermudians since its redis-covery in 1951 and is now protected by law. The birds' dramatic demise occurred with the arrival of a new predator, man, in 1615, who soon made the birds part of their staple diet, with the cahow population, which was once around 50,000 strong, believed to have become extinct by 1650.

Below: *Stretches of the old Bermudian railway line have been transformed into the leafy Railway Trail coastal walk.*

Hamilton Parish at a Glance

BEST TIMES TO VISIT

If you want to take advantage of the water sports and diving on offer at Grotto Bay then visit between May and October when the sea is warm. Outside the main season you may well have many of the parish's attractions to yourself. The Aquarium, zoo and museum complex is busy at any time of year, as Bermudians like to take their children here.

GETTING THERE

Bus numbers 1, 3, 10 and 11, which run between the City of Hamilton and St George, pass through Hamilton Parish. These buses also stop at the airport. The parish can also easily be reached by taxi.

GETTING AROUND

All of the buses listed in the 'Getting There' section drop off and pick up at Grotto Bay, from where you can walk to Blue Hole Park and the Crystal and Fantasy Caves. The same buses also stop at the Aquarium, Zoo and Natural History Museum in Flatts Village. Taxis often wait outside the Grotto Bay Beach Resort, but if there are no cars available then the doorman will ring one for you. Mopeds can be hired from Wheels Cycles, which is situated next to the Shell garage. Those who are unfamiliar with this type of transport should

remember not to drive too close to the walls of the causeway.

WHERE TO STAY

MID-RANGE

Grotto Bay Beach Resort, 11 Blue Hole Hill, tel: 293-8333, fax: 293-2306, www.grotto bay.com Located across the causeway from the airport, this friendly and unpretentious resort hotel is a great first night or family option. A heated outdoor pool, garden jacuzzi, fitness centre, a small private beach and a raft of daily activities (including cave swimming) mean that there is plenty to keep everyone occupied. The hotel also has its own restaurants and bar.
The Clear View Suites, Sandy Lane, tel: 293-0484, fax: 293-0267. Twelve suites and villas complete with their own kitchenettes, the latter also benefit from a separate living area. The dramatic cliff-side location treats guests to impressive Atlantic views. Although guests stay on a room only basis, the suites are adjacent to the Landfall Restaurant. Laundry facilities, tennis court, swimming pools and an on-site art gallery are added attractions.

BUDGET

Domaine Apartments, 43 Old Road, tel: 293-2449, fax: 293-4695, www.domaine

decouto.com Located in Shelly Bay, these studio apartments have TVs, microwaves and oven hobs. There is also free Internet access and a private beach.

Brightside Guest Apartments, 38 North Shore Road, tel: 292-8410, fax: 295-6965, www.bermuda.com/bright side Rooms and cottages accommodating two to eight people, located a short walk from the aquarium.

WHERE TO EAT

LUXURY

Tom Moore's Tavern, Walsingham Lane, tel: 293-8020, www.tommoores.com Bermuda's oldest restaurant has been serving up delicious food for over a century. Enjoy the likes of red snapper and beef fillet on the graceful waterside terrace. On cooler winter evenings dining moves inside to four traditionally styled rooms. A seamless experience, perhaps the finest in Bermuda.

MID-RANGE

Grotto Bay (see Grotto Bay Beach Resort). The hotel has three restaurants, which are open to non-residents. Enjoy casual and relaxed dining amid the palm trees of the appositely named Palm Court, or opt for more formal dining in the elegant Hibiscus Room.

Hamilton Parish at a Glance

Rustico, 8 North Shore Road, tel: 295-5212. This Italian-owned restaurant brings a slice of the Mediterranean to Flatts Village, with fresh fish dishes, light lunches and pasta and pizza staples.

Landfall Restaurant, 161 North Shore Road, tel: 293-1322. Bermudian and international cuisine served in a traditional stone cottage with ocean views. The fried fish and hearty steaks are particularly recommended.

BUDGET
Swizzle Inn, 3 Blue Hole Hill, tel: 293-1854. The inn has become something of a tourist attraction in its own right, and is worth visiting to try the eponymous cocktail or to look at the graffiti-strewn walls alone. Gargantuan portions of hearty bar food like nachos and burgers ensure that you won't leave this Bermuda institution hungry (see page 60).

Bailey's Ice Cream, Blue Hole Hill, tel: 293-9333. This low-key ice-cream parlour is a popular spot when the mercury rises. It also serves simple sandwiches.

Café Ole (see Crystal Caves page 58). This informal cafeteria adjacent to the Crystal Caves is a good place to grab a cooked breakfast, bagel, pastry or a sandwich.

They also serve a large variety of hot and cold drinks.

Four Star Pizza, 6 North Shore Road, tel: 292- 9111. This takeaway restaurant also offers free delivery between the airport and Brighton Hill. An extensive pizza menu is complemented by the option to make up your own. The menu also features chicken wings, sandwiches and a few oriental dishes.

Big Mama's Village Grill, 6 North Shore Road, tel: 296-3634. This small restaurant is open for breakfast, lunch and dinner and serves quite an eclectic array of dishes including light snacks, burgers and Indian dishes.

SHOPPING
Railway Museum & Curiosity Shop (see page 62). Browse the curios on sale in the former waiting room of the railway station, including coloured bottles, Bermuda paraphernalia and books about the British Royal Family.
Bermuda Glass-blowing Studio, 16 Blue Hole Hill, tel: 293-2234. This working studio offers decorative glass-ware at reasonable prices. Shoppers are also invited to watch glass-blowing demon-strations for a nominal fee.

TOURS AND EXCURSIONS
Triangle Diving, 11 Blue Hole Hill, Grotto Bay Beach Resort,

tel: 293-7319, www.triangle diving.com Offering a variety of dives and taster sessions for novices.
Bermuda Bell Diving, Flatts Village, tel: 535-8707, www.helmetdive.com Walk alongside shallow reefs wearing an old-fashioned diving helmet, perfect for those not keen on scuba diving. You can even purchase a video of your trip.
Blue Hole Water Sports, 11 Blue Hole Hill, Grotto Bay Beach Resort, tel: 293-2915, www.blueholewater.bm This company rents out wind surfboards, sailboats and motorboats, as well as snorkel masks and fins. They also have ocean kayaks (which you sit on top of) for one or two people and sunkats (which are similar to pedalos but have motorized engines instead of pedals. The limestone caves around Grotto Bay make this a particularly good snorkelling venue. Hotel guests can swim in the caves as part of an organized activity.

USEFUL CONTACTS
Wheels Cycles, 17 Blue Hole Hill, tel: 293-2378, www.wheelscycles.com Offering moped and scooter hire.
Tucker's Point Club, tel: 298-6970, www.tuckerspoint.com
Mid Ocean Golf Course, tel: 293-0330, www.themid oceanclubbermuda.com

5
Smith's Parish

Smith's Parish, which occupies the stretch of hilly land that lies southwest of the **Harrington Sound** inlet (a large saltwater lake that is fed directly from the sea), owes its name to the former British Ambassador to Russia, Sir Thomas Smith (1588–1625). Although he was the main shareholder in what was dubbed Smith's Tribe by the first settlers, the lord never visited the islands in which he invested so much money, which could be why Bermuda's early residents often called the parish Harris's Bay instead. Smith's is also home to Bermuda's highest point, The Peak, which stands at 79m (259ft); it is also the smallest and one of the least heralded of Bermuda's parishes.

Smith's does, however, have two must-see attractions in the islands' largest protected nature reserve at **Spittal Pond**, with its flocks of migratory birds and stretch of impressive coastline, and the elegant **Verdmont Museum**, one of the best-preserved traditional Bermudian buildings.

These attractions are backed up by some good beaches on the south shore – **John Smith's Bay** is the obvious stand-out – as well as Bermuda's smaller aquarium at **Devil's Hole** and the nefarious delights of the islands' only **microbrewery** in the parish's south-western corner.

DON'T MISS

*** Spittal Pond Nature Reserve: enjoy a tranquil coastal walk, engage in a spot of bird watching or look at the dramatic rocks in Bermuda's largest nature reserve.
*** Verdmont Museum: one of the most important historical houses in Bermuda.
*** John Smith's Bay Park: take a dip in the sea or relax on this attractive beach's pink sands.
*** North Rock Brewing Company: try the island's local ales.

Spittal Pond Nature Reserve ***
This protected 23ha (59-acre) slice of unspoilt coastal Bermuda is a favourite with keen ornithologists, pre-

Opposite: *The tranquil Spittal Pond Nature Reserve.*

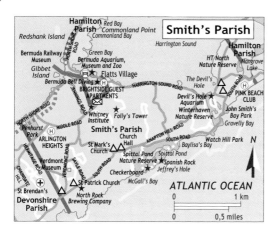

senting Bermuda's best bird watching opportunities. It is also popular with casual walkers and history buffs. Depending on when you visit there may only be a few ducks and other small birds around or, if you are here at the height of the annual migrations in spring and autumn, there can be hundreds of species passing through. The exposed reserve is now fully up and running again after being badly hit during the high winds of Hurricane Fabian in 2003.

Follow the trail from the car park at the western side of the reserve and after negotiating a small farm (something of a rarity in land-hungry Bermuda) and a flurry of trees you come to the **Checkerboard**, a series of limestone rocks that have been carved into weird shapes by the combined efforts of wind, rain and ocean spray. This is a pleasant spot to sit for a while and take in the singing of the birds and the pounding of the Atlantic breakers on the cliffs below; be careful not to get too close to the edge as people have slipped down

Opposite: *The pink sand and craggy rock beauty of John Smith's Bay Park, haunt of the hardy 'Polar Bears' who are renowned locally for their year-round swimming.*
Below: *Sea cliffs at Spittal Pond afford dramatic views east over the Atlantic.*

the rocks in the past. Descend from here and the **reserve's twin ponds** emerge with their busy bird life. You can often spot bright yellow **kiskadees**, **ducks**, **terns**, **owls** and **longtails** as well as some more unusual species brought in, like the first human settlers, after being blown off course in a violent storm.

Seawards from here a path veers off to an old cave, **Jeffrey's**

Cave, where an escaped slave is once said to have hidden away, and then leads on to the spot where a Spanish adventurer – some sources say a humble Portuguese sailor – carved his initials (TF) into the rock, hence its name, **Spanish Rock**, and the date, 1543. This is the oldest sign of human presence in Bermuda, though what you see today is just a replica after attempts to preserve the original led to it crumbling away. It is open sunrise to sunset. Visitors are strongly urged to keep to the pathways to aid the protection of the reserve.

John Smith's Bay Park ★★
This small coastal park is home to one of the nicest beaches in Bermuda, which is open to the public in all its pink sand and cragged rock beauty – popular with photographers all through the year. Right next to the road, this is a great stop on a moped and offers relatively safe year-round paddling and snorkelling for those from climes cold enough to enjoy winter swimming. You will be in good company as a local

> **SWIM LIKE A LOCAL**
>
> In winter locals say it is easy to spot the tourists as they are the only ones daft enough to take on the chilly seas. Most locals stop swimming at the end of September and usually only think of plunging back in for a summer of swimming around Bermuda Day on 24 May. The winter water temperatures of approximately 20°C (68°F) are by no means considered cold by many Europeans and US East-Coasters, so it is easy to see why so many visitors do still choose to swim.

club, the 'Polar Bears', are renowned for their year-round ocean dips. Thanks to the beach's relatively benign nature it is popular with families, though note that there is no lifeguard on duty out of season from October–May. Note also that the beach is reasonably easy to access for disabled people.

Verdmont Museum ***

One of the most delightful buildings in Bermuda has been open to the public since the 1950s as a museum run by the Bermuda National Trust. The building is little changed in 300 years, both in terms of appearance and atmosphere. You cannot miss it as you approach, with its quartet of vaulting chimneys, designed to give heat to each of its eight rooms, looming above as you come down the flower-fringed path.

Below: *Owned by the Bermuda National Trust, Verdmont House is one of Bermuda's best preserved traditional buildings. It also houses an interesting museum.*

The setting of the house is impressive as Verdmont enjoys a lush piece of high ground on Collector's Hill up from the South Road and has its own gardens and sweeping views of the South Shore. It was built way back in 1710 by John Dickinson, a local shipping

magnate, and has somehow managed to avoid being rebuilt and drastically altered over the centuries, making it a real historic piece that offers a glimpse into 18th-century Bermuda. Perhaps the most famous resident was John Green, a judge serving with the Vice-Admiralty Court, who had a big hand in the privateering 'business', which saw 'enemy' ships stripped of their cargos as they tried to pass through Bermudian waters. Fine china abounds and the spoils of privateering are also to be seen, even in the building's construction, which uses solid Georgian pine to back up the elegant Bermudian cedar. The staircase is particularly attractive. Green was also a portrait painter and between 1765 and 1775 he crafted many of the old family portraits that hang from the walls. They depict the ship owner Thomas Smith as well as his four daughters, Mary (Green's wife), Honora, Elizabeth and Catherine. Keeping a watchful eye is Smith's father-in-law, who links back to the original owner as he was married to Elizabeth, the granddaughter of John Dickinson.

Much of the furniture was crafted from Bermudian cedar between 1700 and 1820; highlights include three tallboys, the earliest dating from before the building of Verdmont itself. It is markedly different from the tallboy that dates from the Chippendale period in the 1760s.

Other treasures include the well-preserved doll's house in the attic. If it looks familiar it should do as it is a scale replica of Verdmont House itself, and shows how little it has changed over the years. Other mysterious treasures may have lain within the old chests that were once shipped around by colourful old sea captains, and there are English, French and Chinese versions on show. Open Tuesday–Saturday 10:00–16:00, tel: 236-7369.

Devil's Hole Aquarium *

This aquarium is not nearly as impressive as Bermuda's main aquarium in Hamilton Parish and it is closed in winter, but if you are staying in Smith's Parish and looking for something to do it is a good way to spend an hour

BERMUDA BLOB

In 1998 a strange and giant carcass, which was reputed to measure almost 1m (3ft) by 2.5m (8ft), washed ashore in Bermuda's Mangrove Bay. Its discoverer, Teddy Tucker, reported that the remains looked like a deformed star. As talk of the mysterious find grew, it became known as the 'Bermuda Blob' and has gained something of a cult status as a great sea monster, though the remnants of the mollusc itself have floated back out to sea.

BIGGER AND BETTER?

Controversy surrounds the introduction of so-called mega-cruise ships or Panamax. Some in the tourism ministry sees these mammoth vessels as crucial to the future of Bermuda tourism, while others think their visits will saturate the island and its infrastructure with too many visitors at one time and also have serious environmental impacts. The latter argument includes the widening of the 'Town Cut' to allow these huge vessels in, which campaigners say would irrevocably change Bermuda's natural balance.

ONIONS

At one time Bermudians were often referred to as 'Onions', due to the fact that high-quality onions were shipped from the islands to America. Ironically Bermuda now imports this root vegetable, but the nickname appears to have stuck. You can still find the onion name in surnames and businesses around the island.

or so. Named for the scary sounds the sea makes as it pushes through the hole of the same name, Devil's Hole is actually one of the oldest tourist attractions in Bermuda, first opening its doors as far back as 1834.

The aquarium is connected to Harrington Sound so it offers real sea water, which the resident turtles, sharks and brightly coloured fish seem to enjoy. It is built around a collapsed cave, which forms its own natural aquarium 10m (32ft) deep. Visitors can also buy food and feed some of the marine life. On Tuesday and Friday evenings they often run 'Bermuda Nights' with a guided tour and buffet served. Open daily 09:30–16:30 (summer only).

North Rock Brewing Company

It may never win any international awards, but Bermuda's only microbrewery is well worth a visit if you like your beer. Inside it is all hardwood and cosy snugs with a real pub feel, the perfect place to hang out on a bad weather day, but when the sun shines there is also a terrace that fills up quickly. The food is good and hearty with some healthy options too, but it is the brews that people really come for.

The best way to sample the brewery's impressive range

Below: *Sample the wares at the North Rock Brewing Company, Bermuda's only microbrewery.*

is to try the tasting menu, which is great value at five small glasses of their brews for under $6. There is the Whale of the Wheel (a refreshingly light beer accompanied by a slice of lemon), St David's Light (a tasty golden pilsner), Somers' Amber Ale (a quite malty ale that is similar to an English bitter), Trunk Island Pale Ale (a fruity India pale ale) and North Rock Porter (a dark London porter not a million miles from Guinness).

Smith's Parish at a Glance

BEST TIMES TO VISIT

From the middle of May to late September the gorgeous pink beaches that fringe Smith's Parish fill up with Bermudians and visitors seeking to cool off in the sea. From October to December the sea is still pleasantly warm, but the beaches are almost deserted. Smith's is primarily a residential area and its attractions, setting the beaches aside, are not usually busy regardless of the season.

GETTING THERE

Bus number 1, which runs from the City of Hamilton to St George via the airport, skirts along Smith's Parish's southern coast. Bus route 3 also stops close to Spittal Pond Nature Reserve.

GETTING AROUND

Bus number 1, taxis, bicycles, scooters and mopeds are all ways of getting around Smith's. If you don't have your own wheels then you will need to walk up the hill from the Speciality Inn to the Verdmont Museum.

WHERE TO STAY

Pink Beach Club, 116 South Road, tel: 293-1666, fax: 293-8935, www.pinkbeach. com The elegant cottage colony basks in an enviable location overlooking two private beaches. Sea-view rooms are worth the extra charge, with the Ambassador and Governor suites boasting spacious ocean-front terraces and separate living areas. Free snorkel gear, Internet access, an outdoor swimming pool and television room help keep children happy. Dining options close to the hotel are limited so guests should consider purchasing a meal plan.

WHERE TO EAT

North Rock Brewing Company, 10 South Road, tel: 236-6633, www.northrock brewingcompany.com Bermuda's only microbrewery is also a popular dining spot. At lunch times the diners tend to congregate outside on a shady terrace as they feast on salads, burgers and steak sandwiches. The menu is more sophisticated though and offers the likes of clams steamed in real ale, surf and turf, and a seafood medley of snapper, scallops and shrimps. If you are hankering after fish deep-fried in beer batter and washed down with real ale then this is the place to head for.

Speciality Inn Restaurant, 4 South Road, tel: 236-3133. This local eatery offers a diverse menu. Early morning patrons tuck into American-style cooked breakfasts of eggs, ham, omelettes, hash browns, pancakes and waffles. Breakfast sandwiches and pastries are available for those looking for a lighter breakfast, with meal combos catering to the famished. If you want to try a traditional Bermudian breakfast of codfish and potato then come here between 06:00 and 11:30 on Saturdays. At lunch time salads, soups, sandwiches, burgers and pasta dominate the menu, while dinner is a hearty affair with fish and chips, curried mussels, and pizza also on offer. If this isn't enough then the restaurant also serves sushi.

Bermudiana Restaurant (see Pink Beach Club). This formal fine-dining restaurant offers a good value five-course menu and stunning Atlantic views, which are best enjoyed from the outdoor terrace on warm summer evenings.

USEFUL CONTACTS

Wheels Cycles, 116 South Road, tel: 292-0388.
Bermuda Bell Diving, Flatts Village, tel: 535-8707, www.helmetdive.com Although officially located in Hamilton Parish, Bermuda Bell Diving is easily accessible from Smith's Parish. The company takes clients for a walk along a shallow reef wearing old-fashioned diving helmets.
Kiteski Bermuda, Flatts Village, tel: 735-8164. This Hamilton Parish operation is tantalizingly close to Smith's and offers water-skiing and parasailing.

6
Devonshire Parish

Devonshire Parish, which lies in a central position, with its rolling hills connecting the west and east ends of Bermuda, is a mainly residential parish, which is often overlooked by visitors. Once Devonshire was dominated by marshland, but man has clawed back much of the land over the centuries.

Devonshire may not boast an array of famous sights, nor glorious beaches to lure tourists, but it has a relaxed charm that is enhanced by the gorgeous gardens of **Palm Grove**, the leafy **Arboretum** and the pleasant coastal **Devonshire Bay Park**. Then there are the historic buildings of **Palmetto House** and the **Old Devonshire Church**, which neatly sum up the sort of understated refinement that characterizes the parish.

To those who know anything about William Cavendish, the first Earl of Devonshire (1552–1626), it seems fitting that the parish should have acquired the name of what historical sources refer to as a true gentleman, a wealthy aristocrat who didn't let his enormous personal wealth and position in society go to his head. Sadly Cavendish never made it to Bermuda, dying at Hardwick Hall in Devonshire in 1626, at the age of 73.

Devonshire Bay Park ***
This pleasant little coastal park looks out across pretty Devonshire Bay and into the Atlantic. It is a lofty spot, a fact not missed by the British who plonked a battery up here during the American Civil War when

Don't Miss

*** **Palm Grove Garden:** elegant gardens complete with moongates, ponds and a relief of Bermuda.
** **Old Devonshire Church:** this attractive whitewashed church is one of the oldest on the islands.
* **Devonshire Bay Park:** atmospheric ruins in a spot overlooking the ocean.
* **Arboretum:** enjoy a leisurely walk amongst indigenous and imported trees.
* **Palmetto House and Park:** traditional 'cross house' in attractive grounds.

Opposite: *A sea breeze blows through the trees at Devonshire Bay Park.*

they feared an impending attack. There are no big guns or museum exhibits here, instead just the rough-hewn rock that you can walk through and conjure up images of the men who used to man the fortifications, which were active right up until the end of World War II. On windy days the surf dramatically pounds the cliffs below; when the sea is calmer fishermen try their luck, but visitors should beware of being knocked off their feet when the surf is up.

Palm Grove Garden ***

The ultra-rich family that own this elegant park, the Gibbons, no longer allow unfettered daily access, but at least the gardens are still open to the public four days a week. The highlight for many visitors is the pond that hosts a map of Bermuda, complete with many of its islands, laid out in grass in the middle of the water, but the rest of the gardens are even more impressive.

Approach from the west and you enter through the Chinese moongate, where you can make a wish as you pass. A lovely walkway leads off to an ornate pond, before you head up the hill southwards to the larger pond with a Bermuda relief. The gardens are awash with cute little flourishes – statues dotted around amongst the lush plants, shrubs and trees – as well as a collection of colourful tropical birds. Views of the Atlantic also open up from the gardens on the other side of the house. Open Monday–Thursday 08:00–17:00.

Old Devonshire Church ★★

Located just past the New Devonshire Church, this quaint little place of worship is one of the oldest on the islands. It first opened its doors back in 1716 on the site of an earlier church and its appearance has changed little since, despite it having to be largely rebuilt following an explosion at Easter in 1970. (The New Devonshire Church, which was built in the 19th century, is also worth popping into, as it is a more striking and much taller building.)

The graveyard is full of interesting old headstones, many dating back to the 18th and 19th centuries. Look out for the large family vaults, which descend deep below the ground, saving precious space as they go. Inside the whitewashed church itself is a collection of 16th-century silver that survived the explosion, though its opening hours are irregular and it is not always possible to get in. Throughout the year the church hosts a number of special services, which can be a moving experience whether you are a believer or not. Some of the services are candlelit, creating a magical ambience.

Nearby **Devonshire Marsh** may not be quite as impressive or visitor-friendly as Paget, but ornithologists may want to visit for its migratory birds, though it does not have a marked walkway to help you along.

THE FAMOUS PRINCESS

The Hamilton Princess is easily Bermuda's most historic hotel. Named in honour of Princess Louise, whose sojourn on Bermuda helped kick-start its tourist industry, the Princess opened her elegant doors in January 1885. This was Mark Twain's favourite Bermudian place to roll up a cigar and take in the view from the veranda. In World War II the hotel became a hotbed of espionage as the headquarters of the British Secret Service with over 1,000 workers beavering away in the basement.

Below: *An ornate pond in Palm Grove Garden, a private estate owned by the Gibbons family but open to the public from Monday to Thursday.*

Arboretum *

The 8ha (20-acre) arboretum may be a little shabby these days, with missing signposts and dirty tracks leading off through the trim grass, but its collection of trees is a wonderful testimony to Bermuda's fertile climate and fine growing conditions. Run by the Department of Agriculture, the park was first established for the purposes of experiment and research in the 1950s, with saplings brought in from as far afield as the Royal Botanical Gardens at Kew in London.

As well as a host of indigenous trees – including native palmetto palms and Bermuda's famous cedar – look out also for ebony and rubber trees. The park is a favourite with rule-breaking local kids looking for somewhere to kick their footballs around. Open daily sunrise to sunset.

Palmetto House and Park *

The Palmetto House is a lovely little historical house that reclines in a web of vegetation just off the North Shore Road. Run by the Bermuda National Trust, its bleached white façade is striking, while indoors you can admire the impressive staircase and solid antique furnishings. The design of the house is of the traditional 'cross house' variety, so named because the structure is shaped like a cross.

If you are in the mood for a stroll afterwards head west into Palmetto Park, a good 7ha (17-acre) spot for a picnic, or neighbouring **Robinson Bay Park**, which fronts the ocean. If you fancy an even longer walk, a pleasant stretch of the **Railway Trail** heads east for a couple of miles from near Palmetto House up to Flatts where you can easily catch a bus back to Palmetto or directly on to Hamilton. Interesting sights along the route include views out to **Gibbet Island**, where those accused of witchcraft were once burned at the stake, and the relaxed **Penhurst Park** with its walking trails and swimming.

Below: *The attractive whitewashed Palmetto House, managed by the Bermuda National Trust, is constructed in a traditional 'cross house' design.*

Devonshire Parish at a Glance

Best Times to Visit

This laid-back residential parish is enjoyable to visit at any time of year. From September to May when the humidity is lower you can really spend time exploring the public parks and elegant Palm Grove Gardens, although the grounds of this private estate are only open to the public from Monday to Thursday. Any keen golfers who are in Bermuda between November and March should head to the Ocean View Golf Course on Mondays for the Visitor Golf Tournament.

Getting There

Bus numbers 10 and 11, which link the City of Hamilton and St George, run along Devonshire's North Shore Road, with the former diverting down Palmetto Road into Pembroke. Bus route 3 will take you to any destination along Middle Road, with route number 1 serving the South Road.

Getting Around

The Ocean View Golf Course and Palmetto Park and Palmetto House can be reached by taking buses 10 and 11 along the North Shore, with bus route three dropping passengers by the Old Devonshire Church and the Arboretum; for South Shore destinations hop on bus number 1.

Where to Stay

Luxury
Ariel Sands Beach Club, 34 South Road, tel: 236-1010, fax: 236-0087, www.arielsands.com This prestigious beach-front cottage colony has 46 elegantly furnished rooms and suites, two saltwater swimming pools, heated freshwater pool, tennis courts, fitness centre, spa, private beach and a hot tub overlooking the Atlantic. The property is also home to one of Bermuda's most highly regarded restaurants.

Budget
Burch's Guest Apartments, 110 North Shore Road, tel: 292-5746, fax: 295-3794. This relaxed guesthouse has self-contained apartments that come complete with two double beds, a fully equipped kitchen, air-conditioning and satellite TV. A small outdoor pool and garden with panoramic North Shore sea views enhance the appeal.

Where to Eat

Luxury
Aqua (see Ariel Sands). A winner of prestigious local awards, this fine-dining restaurant offers a fusion menu that features Thai, Indian, Oriental and Caribbean dishes alongside more traditional European and American fare. Dine on the restaurant's ocean-front terrace or in the attractive nautically themed blue interior. In the main summer period diners retire to the after-dinner lounge for live entertainment.

Shopping

Barn Thrift Shop, 53 Devon Springs Road, tel: 236-3155. After more than 40 years of operation this second-hand charity shop, staffed by volunteers from the Hospitals Auxiliary of Bermuda, has become something of a Bermuda institution, where it is possible to pick up worn but pristine clothing, and other second hand goods for a fraction of their original retail price. Proceeds go to the King Edward VII Memorial Hospital. Call ahead to check current opening hours.

Useful Contacts

The National Equestrian Centre, PO Box DV 583, tel: 234-0485, www.bef.bm Keep your eyes open for dressage, showjumping and pony-racing events, particularly in the summer months.
The National Sports Centre, 50 Frog Lane, tel: 295-8085. Check with your hotel concierge or in the local paper for details about forthcoming football, cricket and rugby games.
Ocean View Golf Course, Barkers Hill, tel: 295-9093. This nine-hole public golf course has commanding views. There are 18 tees for those who want to play a full 18 holes and golf clubs are available to rent.

7
Pembroke Parish

The central parish that includes and surrounds the capital of Hamilton may be mainly residential, but it packs a good slice of history and a number of attractions into its confines. Pembroke Parish also boasts sweeping views across the ocean that take in a panorama as far as the Royal Naval Dockyard on the tip of the West End and St George's Island at the East End.

Just a couple of kilometres east of Hamilton lies the popular **Bermuda Underwater Exploration Institute**, a bright and modern interactive museum far more interesting than its name suggests. Other worthwhile sights include the relaxing little park at **Spanish Point**, **Admiralty Park** and the **Government House**, although the latter is not open to the public.

Bermuda Underwater Exploration Institute ★★★

The motto 'Where Land Ends Exploration Begins' immediately gives you an idea what the Ocean Discovery Centre at the Institute is all about. This well thought out hi-tech experience pleases kids and big kids alike, with rooms stocked full of interactive displays, old diving gear and models. The ground floor houses what has to be one of the world's most impressive collections of shells, with what is on display today only a fraction of the actual treasure-trove amassed by dedicated local enthusiast John Lightbourn. Nearby a short film explores some of the dark tales of the Bermuda Triangle, but rather disappointingly fails to solve the age-old mystery.

DON'T MISS

★★★ **Bermuda Underwater Exploration Institute:** this interactive museum is great for kids and big kids alike.
★★ **Government House:** take a sneaky look at how the other half live.
★★★ **Spanish Point Park:** this tranquil coastal park is a great place to watch the windsurfers, or to simply enjoy the views across the Great Sound to the Royal Naval Dockyard.

Opposite: *Government House, one of Bermuda's most impressive buildings.*

The highlight for younger visitors is the 'dive' thousands of feet down to the depths of the ocean floor. The simulated submersible – actually a lift programmed to judder and shake its way to the lower level of the museum – is a ride that can be a little scary for really young ones as it 'malfunctions', is attacked by an admittedly unconvincing giant squid and then the call goes out to abandon ship. On the lower level more displays await, including a 'Treasure Room' and a simulated shark tank, which are both appealing for children. For the grown-ups there is the rather sophisticated La Coquille Restaurant (*see page 87*). Look out also for lectures and various other events throughout the year at this very active non-profit institute. Open Monday–Friday 09:00–17:00, Saturday–Sunday 10:00–17:00.

CHILDREN

Bermuda is well set-up for children. The beaches are very popular with younger visitors and many restaurants are more than happy to cater for their demands, though check at the more expensive eateries. Many of the big resort hotels have programmes for children that help give parents a rest.

Government House ★★

The grounds of the rather grand Government House are no longer open to visitors, perhaps a wise move by the authorities after the slaying in 1973 of governor Sir Richard Sharples, his bodyguard and his pet dog. You can, though, drive up to the gates and garner a fair idea of how the other half lives – the other half that includes visiting British royalty (Prince Andrew visited in 2005) as well as the governor himself. The actual building, which enjoys a prime spot on a hill with sweeping views of the islands and the ocean, dates back to the tail end of the 19th century, though the trees that dot the grounds are a bit more eclectic, as visiting dignitaries are encouraged to bring along their own choice of tree, which all seem to be flourishing rather well in the mild, frost-free Bermuda climate.

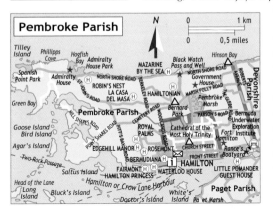

Pembroke Parish

Black Watch Pass and Well *

Dedicated to the efforts of the famous Scottish Regiment, these projects show the difficulties man has encountered in nurturing life on Bermuda. The well was dug to relieve a serious drought that threatened the islands back in 1849, though some locals insist that no drop of water was ever drawn from it. Black Watch Pass, meanwhile, is a dramatic road cut right through the voluminous limestone rocks that separate Pembroke Parish from the islands' capital.

Admiralty House and Park *

The tumbledown Admiralty House may not be much to look at these days, but it boasts an interesting history. Before this 19th-century building housed the admiral himself, who oversaw all of the British Navy's operations in the region, it served as a naval hospital. From the house a path leads off through the 6ha (16 acre) grounds. To the northeast, continue through some dense foliage and you soon emerge at the small, sheltered Clarence Cove, which has a modest little beach that is popular in summer. There are a couple of benches where you can sit and stare out at the ocean and the yachts bobbing in the distance.

Opposite: *John Lightbourn's shell collection on display at the Bermuda Underwater Exploration Institute.*
Below: *It may be a little dilapidated today, but Admiralty House is still worth a visit.*

WATER SPORTS

Bermuda is justifiably popular with lovers of all sorts of water sports. Here you can go out on everything from a canoe or a wind surfboard right through to a speedboat. Numerous operators service the islands so just check at local tourist offices or your hotel for details; many hotels can book water-sports activities with other operators if they do not have anything on site.

Below: *Spanish Point Park takes its name from the Spanish sailors who were shipwrecked here.*

Spanish Point Park ★★

One of the windiest points in the islands is an obvious favourite with windsurfers and you can also see the bigger yachts from here, sailing around the coastal waters. The park gets its name from the Spanish sailors, under the command of Captain Diego Ramirez, who were shipwrecked here way back in the 17th century just before Somers' fateful arrival. They set up camp at this spot while they made rapid repairs to their ship, noting the plentiful supply of birds to feast on, and while they were soon on their way – fleeing the islands that the Spanish feared due to their supposed demons – the first British arrivals soon after found evidence of their visit, hence the name. Local legend has it that they left a sign pointing to the source of fresh water to help newcomers – a sign the British misunderstood and so spent hours in a fruitless search for buried treasure.

Skulking in the water at the entrance to the small

craft harbour by the point are the rusting remnants of an old dry dock that was actually towed all the way across the Atlantic (it took over a month for four powerful ships to haul it) from its birthplace in the River Thames in the 19th century. Many people, including locals, wrongly presume it is a shipwreck, but a plaque nearby sets anyone interested straight. Attempts were actually made to haul it off for scrap, but it broke into pieces whilst being towed and now seems destined to remain half submerged at this scenic spot.

Pembroke Parish at a Glance

Weatherwise Pembroke is at its best when the sun is out and the aquamarine sea that fringes the parish's north and south shores is at its most dazzling. From November through to March you are likely to have both the main sights and the parish's hidden treasures virtually to yourself. If you want to combine a visit to the Bermuda Underwater Exploration Institute and La Coquille, note that the restaurant is closed on Sundays.

Bus number 4 runs through the parish, which can also be reached on bus routes number 10 and 11, as well as by taxi, moped or bicycle.

Many of the sights in Pembroke can be reached on foot from the City of Hamilton, as can the apartments and restaurants listed here. Alternatively bus route 4 runs to Spanish Point and along the North Shore, while routes 10 and 11 run up Blackwatch Pass.

Accommodation on Pembroke's North Shore is listed here, while establishments closer to the City of Hamilton are listed on pages 40–41.
BUDGET
La Casa Del Masa, 7 Eve's Hill Lane, tel: 292-8726, fax: 295-4447. Each of these spacious

self-contained suites on Pembroke's North Shore has two double beds and a separate kitchen. Guests can also use the small outdoor pool.

Mazarine By The Sea, 91 North Shore Road, tel: 292-1960, fax: 292-9077, www.mazarineby thesea.com Rooms at this small guesthouse are clean and have commanding sea views. A small pool area also looks out over the North Shore and there is easy access to the sea.

Robin's Nest, 10 Vale Close, North Shore, tel/fax: 292-4347. These self-contained air-conditioned apartments come complete with their own kitchens and access to a large freshwater pool. Rooms sleeping two, three and four people are available, as are extra beds for children under the age of 12.

Hamiltonian Hotel & Island Club, 6 Robin Hood Drive, tel: 295-5608, fax: 295-7481. This small pink hotel has equally pink guestrooms, which are simply furnished and come complete with a microwave, toaster, coffee maker and fridge. There is also a large outdoor pool and three tennis courts for guests to enjoy.

La Coquille Restaurant & Bar, Bermuda Underwater Exploration Institute, 40

Crow Lane, tel: 292-6122. For fine French cuisine served up in a hard-to-beat location head here. The stylish white interior and stunning views over Hamilton Bay merit a visit to La Coquille alone. The restaurant participates in a winter dine around scheme (*see* panel, page 25). The majority of shops in Pembroke Parish are located in the City of Hamilton (*see* page 41).

The Bermuda Underwater Exploration Institute (*see* page 83). The gift shop at the BUEI has a small but tasteful selection of marine-themed gifts.

A large number of grocery stores are also located in the parish:
Arnold's Family Market, 113 St John's Road, tel: 292-3310.
C-Mart, 96 North Shore Road, tel: 292-5332.
Happy Valley Mini Mart, Happy Valley Road, tel: 292-1197.
Manuel Soares & Son, 1 Old House Lane, tel: 292-1426.
Miles Market, 96 Pitt's Bay Road, tel: 295-1234.
The Garden Market, 13 Serpentine Road, tel: 292-7000.

See the City of Hamilton at a Glance (pages 40–41).

8
Paget Parish

Paget Parish is one of the most popular residential areas in Bermuda, with a flurry of expensive homes lining the waterfront that gazes towards Hamilton. It is easy to catch a bus or ferry right into Hamilton, transport links are also good with the rest of Bermuda, and there are plenty of hotels and restaurants, making it a good base for tourism.

While the commuters enjoy their lavish residences on the North Shore, the interior holds the virgin land of **Paget Marsh** and the lush **Botanical Gardens**, two of Bermuda's top sights, as well as the historic houses of **Waterville** and **Camden**, the **Museum of Bermuda Art** and, in the shape of **Elbow Beach** on the South Shore, one of Bermuda's finest and most popular beaches.

Botanical Gardens and Camden House ★★★

These lush subtropical gardens are a wonderful place to relax and take a stroll. There is no entry charge to the 15ha (36-acre) site, which has managed to recover from the ravages of Hurricane Fabian in 2003 with a minimum of fuss. Many visitors just scramble around to look at the various species and their well-marked descriptions, but the best way to really get a feel for the place is by going on one of the free one-and-a-half-hour guided tours on Tuesdays, Wednesdays and Fridays.

Opened at the tail end of the 19th century as an experiment to determine what could grow on Bermudian soil, the answer seems to be just about anything. The flora flourishes year-round – everything

ATLANTIC OCEAN
ST GEORGE
St George's
Hamilton
Sandys
Pembroke
HAMILTON
Smith's
Devonshire
Paget
Warwick
Southampton

DON'T MISS
★★★ **Botanical Gardens and Camden House:** learn about Bermuda's indigenous and imported fauna on an engaging guided tour.
★★★ **Paget Marsh:** follow the raised wooden trail over the marsh and get a feel for Bermuda of the past.
★★ **Elbow Beach:** swim, snorkel and sunbathe on one of the islands' most impressive stretches of sand.

Opposite: *The warm orange glow of sunset over Elbow Beach.*

from swaying palms and casuarina trees, through to hulking rubber trees and that Bermudian staple, the cedar, as well as spiky cacti and a technicolor army of hibiscus.

The aforementioned guided tours are the best way to appreciate the breadth of what the gardens hold, and volunteers will enthuse you with their passion for the place. Also make sure to take time to explore the recently opened butterfly garden with its camera-pleasing butterflies, and the 'sensory garden', opened with the blind in mind, but glorious for anyone with its myriad range of aromatic herbs and spices. Open sunrise to sunset.

Just a short stroll from the Botanical Gardens' visitor centre is the grand **Camden House**, an 18th-century building that enjoys sweeping views over the gardens and onto the Atlantic, especially from the two levels of veranda that were added in the 19th century. Camden was brought back to its full glory in the 1970s after years of neglect, in order to serve as the official residence of the Premier, though in reality it is only used for lavish, official government functions when he is looking to impress. Unusually for such a politically important building you can just saunter through taking in the plush surrounds and elegant use of Bermuda cedar (even some of the serving plates are cedar) as various former premiers stare down at you from the walls. Open daily 12:00–14:00.

Masterworks Museum of Bermuda Art *

Near Camden House is this impressive 1000-work art collection. The old building that houses the works is impressive in itself, perhaps more so for those with traditional tastes.

Inside, as well as paintings by some illustrious names, there is also a focus on Bermudian themes by Bermudian painters (the aptly named 'Bringing Art Home' collection) and you can even take a piece back home with you if you really like it and have the money to spare. Patrons of the trust that runs the gallery are said to include Prince Charles. The trust is very active in local cultural affairs with a raft of temporary exhibitions as well as

an 'artist in residence' programme. The trust's new museum is set to open in 2007. Open daily 10:00–18:00, tel: 236-2950, www.bermudamasterworks.com

Above: *Camden House.*
Opposite: *After recovering from the ravages of Hurricane Fabian, the Botanical Gardens are now back to their best.*

Birdsey Studio ★

Art lovers should make a beeline for this small studio. The owner these days is Jo Birdsey Lindberg, daughter of the celebrated Alfred Birdsey (see page 27), who died in 1996 after a lifetime spent capturing the spirit and beauty of Bermuda on canvas – perhaps like no other. While it is his fame that brings most visitors here, Jo is no mean artist either and she has taken on her father's mantle to produce some excellent impressionist work, some of which is on sale. You can

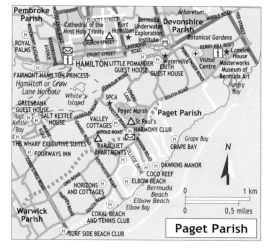

TRIMINGHAM'S

In July 2005, a real Bermudian institution declared itself bankrupt after 163 years of trading. A decline in tourist arrivals, the high costs associated with trading in Bermuda and the rise of e-commerce were among the reasons for the closure, which came just 16 months after Trimingham's merged with rival Smith's to become Trimingham Smith's. Its landmark store on Front Street looks set to become a branch of the Bank of Bermuda.

DISABLED ACCESS

Unlike in the UK and USA there is no legislation forcing businesses to provide disabled access and this is reflective of a destination that is not particularly good for disabled travellers, though there is special provision at the airport. Some hotels do boast specially adapted rooms and restaurants do claim to be disabled-friendly, but there can be a distance between the claims and the reality. For further information, contact organizations for the disabled in your home country or the Bermuda Department of Tourism (see page 122).

also buy small reproductions of Alfred's work. The studio is open Monday–Friday 10:30–13:00, March–July and September–November.

Waterville *

Waterville, a wonderful example of typical Bermudian architecture with its rainwater collecting roofs, pastel pink sheen and sturdy twin chimneys, is one of the oldest houses anywhere on the islands. Built in the early 18th century, Waterville was home to seven generations of the prominent Trimingham family (the famous owners of the now defunct Trimingham's department store on Front Street) until 1990 and today it houses the headquarters of the Bermuda National Trust. You can visit a few of the rooms, which are bedecked in old furniture, photographs and vintage clocks, and pick up more information on the rest of the Trust's properties.

Make sure to also visit the waterfront grounds with their bountiful roses and wooden summerhouse. The benches make an ideal spot for admiring the verdant vegetation and taking in the sea breeze. If you fancy throwing an impressive party they rent out the house

Right: *Wooden gazebo in the gardens of Waterville, the former Trimingham family home.*

and gardens for functions. Open
Monday–Friday 09:00–17:00, tel:
236-6483, http://www.bnt.bm

Paget Marsh ★★★

If you want to know what Bermuda looked, smelled and felt like
before the first settlers scrambled
their way ashore then come to the
green oasis of Paget Marsh. A
raised wooden walkway straddles
one of the last few remaining tracts
of virgin swamp – most of Bermuda's mosquito-ridden swamps
were soon drained by man. Look
out for the lounging lizards, hunt-

Above: *Raised wooden walkways protect the fauna and flora at Paget Marsh.*

ing herons and singing kiskadee birds as you wander
amongst the 10ha (25 acres) of mangrove, native
palmetto palm and cedar trees that were opened up to
the public in 2000.

Information boards are on hand to give you more
details about the flora and fauna on show. Stick to the
walkway as many of the species here are protected and
have survived precisely because no one has traipsed
over them before.

Elbow Beach ★★

Some visitors are put off visiting popular Elbow Beach
as some of it is reserved for guests of the luxurious
Elbow Beach Hotel, now run by the plush Mandarin
Oriental group. The truth is that there is plenty of
space for everyone and if you are hungry you can
even pop into the hotel at the east end of the sands for
lunch at beachfront Mickey's restaurant in summer.
This is one of Bermuda's finest pink sand beaches,
which are backed by dunes and peppered with small
rocks, and it is justifiably popular amongst early-
morning joggers, enjoying the pink glaze sunrise and
the booming Atlantic breakers. Sunset, however, is
definitely the best time to be here.

CALL OF THE KISKADEE

You will soon find out where
this bird gets its unusual
name from, as its unique
onomatopoeic call echoes
around Bermuda. Follow the
sound and you will find
them reclining in trees, with
their canary yellow plumes
and black heads. They were
originally brought in from
Trinidad in the 1950s in an
effort to wipe out the local
lizard population, and have
never looked back.

Paget Parish at a Glance

Paget's beaches are at their busiest between May and Oct when it is possible to hire water-sports equipment. Between Jun and Sep the sea temperature reaches the mid-20s. The Botanical Gardens and Paget Marsh are attractions that can be enjoyed at any time of year, and on Tue, Wed and Fri between Nov and Mar there are free guided tours of the former.

GETTING THERE

Bus 2 takes you from the City of Hamilton as far as Ord Road, while bus route 8 provides access to the parish from the Royal Naval Dockyard, as well as the islands' capital. The parish's South Shore is accessible on bus number 7, which also runs between the City of Hamilton and the Royal Naval Dockyard. To reach Paget from the north of the island you will need to change buses in the City of Hamilton. Ferries from the capital dock at Lower Ferry, Hodsdon's Ferry, Salt Kettle, Darrell's Wharf and Belmont Ferry.

GETTING AROUND

Taxis and buses are the safest ways to travel around the parish, with moped and scooter hire also available.

WHERE TO STAY

LUXURY
Elbow Beach, 60 South Road,

tel: 239-8900, fax: 239-8906, www.mandarinoriental.com Bermuda's only Leading Hotels of the World resort, which is expertly managed by the Mandarin Oriental group, boasts one of the best stretches of private beach in Bermuda, with a host of water-sports equipment available to rent. Elegant guest rooms, high-quality restaurants and a luxurious spa, with six individual suites, complete the winning combination.
CoCo Reef, 8 College Drive, tel: 236-5416, fax: 236-9766, www.cocoreefbermuda.com This attractive cottage colony set in elegant gardens has 62 ocean-front or ocean-view room and suites. The hotel also has an outdoor pool, two restaurants and a bar.
Coral Beach & Tennis Club, 34 South Road, tel: 236-2233, fax: 236-1876, www.coralbeachclub.com This private members' club offers luxurious accommodation in Bermudian-style cottages and suites, as well as 32 standard guest rooms. Members also have access to a private beach, a fitness studio, squash and tennis courts and a spa.
Horizons and Cottages, 33 South Road, tel: 236-0048, fax: 236-1981, www.horizons cottages.com The oldest cottage colony in Bermuda is pleasantly small-scale and is part of the esteemed Relais & Châteaux brand. Guests can

choose to stay in the main house, as well as the graceful cottages and suites; they also have access to the facilities at the private members' Coral Beach and Tennis Club.
Fourways Inn, 1 Middle Road, tel: 236-6517, fax: 236-5528, www.fourwaysinn.com Known more for its food than its accommodation, this inn also has an intimate and exclusive cottage colony with just 11 suites.

MID-RANGE
Grape Bay Hotel, 55 White Sands Road, tel: 236-3500, fax: 236-2486 www.bermuda resorthotels.com Recently reopened after an extensive renovation and a change of name, the hotel has spacious rooms decorated with Bermudian flair. If your budget can stretch to it, book a superior sea-view room. Some good rates available.
Harmony Club, 109 South Road, tel: 236-3500, fax: 236-2624, www.bermudaresort hotels.com Until 2005 the cottage-style Harmony Club was an all-inclusive property; today accommodation is on a room-only basis, which brings its rates down to the budget level between Nov and Jan.
The Wharf Executive Suites, 1 Harbour Road, tel: 232-5700, fax: 232-4008, www.wharf executivesuites.com Geared towards those visiting Bermuda for an extended period of time, this property comprises large

self-contained suites with kitchen facilities and high-speed Internet access, with the added bonus of a concierge service. Bookings are accepted on a weekly, monthly or yearly basis.

BUDGET

Dawkins Manor Hotel, 29 St Michael's Road, tel: 236-7419, fax: 236-7088, http://bermuda-charm.com This modern property has eight guest suites with fully equipped kitchens and simple bedrooms. Residents can also use the outdoor pool and sun terrace, as well as the guest lounge. Winter rates (Nov–Mar) are particularly good value.
Greenbank Guesthouse, 17 Salt Kettle Road, tel: 236-3615, fax: 236-2427, www.green bankbermuda.com This pleasant guesthouse enjoys an enviable position amidst lush gardens on the western shore of the Salt Kettle Peninsula, overlooking the City of Hamilton and the Great Sound. Choose from a double room or self-contained apart-ments (the majority of which have their own kitchenettes) that sleep up to four people.
Paraquet Apartments Ltd, 72 South Road, tel: 236-5842, fax: 236-1665, www.para quetapartments.com This motel-style accommodation is a decent budget option, but the apartments are situated close to the main road and do not benefit from ocean views.

For those who don't want to self-cater the apartments have their own restaurant and there is also a shop nearby.
Little Pomander Guesthouse, 16 Pomander Road, tel: 236-7635, fax: 236-8332, www.littlepomander.com This attractive waterfront cottage has five comfortable rooms and offers fine harbour views from the small terrace and lawn.

WHERE TO EAT

LUXURY

Seahorse Grill (see Elbow Beach). The menu at this award-winning restaurant features 'New Bermudian' cuisine. Choose from the likes of *foie gras*, duck, Black Angus beef and scallops. An á la carte and fixed price menu are available.

MID-RANGE

Lido Café (see Elbow Beach). Feast on fresh fish, pasta, lobster and tasty grills at this stylish Italian eatery. On warm evenings the restau-rant's Sea Breeze terrace fills with happy diners, with the same spectacular sea views available from the glass fronted exterior.
Mickey's (see Elbow Beach). This informal restaurant is a buzzing beach bistro serving European dishes like shrimp linguine and sirloin steak. Only open during the main tourist season.
Fourways Inn (see Fourways Inn). This fine-dining restau-

rant has achieved almost leg-endary status in Bermuda, with visitors and locals raving about the food, service and Sunday brunch. Between Nov and Mar the restaurant takes part in a good value dine around scheme (see panel, page 25).
Horizons and Cottages (see Horizons and Cottages). The Ocean Terrace and Middleton dining room are open to non-residents.
Jamaican Grill, 33 Ord Road, tel: 232-0420. The Paget branch of this chain of take-away restaurants serves up Jamaican rice and meat dishes.
Juanito's (see CoCo Reef Resort). Dine on meat, fish, poultry and other culinary treats in this stylish ocean-view restaurant.

TOURS AND EXCURSIONS

Discover Bermuda Tours (see Waterville page 192), tel: 236-6483. Offer a guided tour of Waterville and Paget Marsh on Wednesdays from 10:00–12:30.

USEFUL CONTACTS

Blue Water Water Sports & Blue Water Divers, Elbow Beach, tel: 234-1034.
Eve Cycles Ltd, 114 Middle Road, tel: 236-6247.
Elbow Beach Cycles, South Shore Road, tel: 236-9237.
Oleander Cycles, 6 Valley Road, tel: 236-5235.
King Edward VII Memorial Hospital, 7 Point Finger Road, tel: 236-2345.

9
Warwick Parish

Warwick Parish is a beach lovers' fantasy. Its South Shore enchants the eye with sweeping stretches of pink-hued sand, backed up by sea cliffs, with easy access to the turquoise water. If you only visit one parish for its beaches, make it Warwick, taking in Astwood Park as well as the delights of the South Shore Park, which runs west from Warwick into Southampton Parish.

Heading away from the beaches, which is often easier said than done after you have discovered them, Warwick also has a number of other worthwhile places to visit. Nature lovers will enjoy the small protected reserve at **Warwick Pond**, **Christ Church** is one of the prettiest churches in Bermuda, and the parish is also renowned as a great venue for horse-riding and golf.

South Shore Park and Warwick Parish Beaches ★★★

If you have come to Bermuda in search of world-class beaches, fringed by swaying subtropical trees and fronted by the sort of crystal clear waters that you feared might only exist in glossy tourist brochures, then this is definitely the place for you. Drop down from either of the car parks at Warwick Long Bay and you enter a world of glorious beaches, with a web of nature trails linking them (stretching the full one-and-a-half-mile length of the park) and everything from sweeping stretches of sand through to isolated little coves where you can snorkel undisturbed amongst the abundant marine life.

DON'T MISS

★★★ South Shore Park and Warwick Parish Beaches: some of Bermuda's best beaches.
★★ Christ Church: even the austere Presbyterian Church of Scotland has softened in the Bermuda sunshine and the church is painted a pastel pink!
★★ Warwick Pond Nature Reserve: follow the forest trail to learn about the reserve's birds and flora.
★★ Astwood Park: enjoy a picnic as you take in sweeping Atlantic views.

Opposite: *The crystal clear waters of Warwick Parish.*

Above: *The attractive salmon pink façade of the Presbyterian Church of Scotland's Christ Church. Check out the stained-glass windows.*

Warwick Long Bay itself is one of the islands' finest beaches, a half-mile of unbroken, coral-tinged sand. You can often get a bit of surf here – nothing too exciting, but enough to have some fun body-boarding. There are also patches of reef just a short distance offshore that you can head out to if you have your own snorkel mask.

Once you have explored Warwick Long Bay, head further west along the trails that ultimately lead on into Southampton Parish and its beach jewel, Horseshoe Bay. On the way you can wander amid the sandy dunes, stopping off at any cove that takes your fancy. Some of the smaller coves can only be reached by swimming so if you are not carrying too much gear this is the way to escape the summer crowds. Sheltered **Jobson Cove** is one of the highlights for families, a picture-perfect little spot that nestles amongst the rocks just west of Warwick Long Bay. Continue on and you come to equally attractive stretches of beach at **Stonehole Bay** and **Chaplin Bay**.

Christ Church ★★

One of the islands' most striking churches, this branch of the Presbyterian Church of Scotland is one of the oldest Presbyterian churches in the Western Hemisphere. It welcomed its first congregation as far back as 1719 and it is still well attended today, with an active community hall also standing nearby. The salmon pink façade welcomes you into the cool, dark interior – home to a trio of colourful stained-glass windows that lie in its eastern corner, as well as an interesting pulpit. In the graveyard you can spend some time reading the inscriptions that all tell their own tragic stories.

Warwick Pond Nature Reserve ★★

It may not be quite as impressive as its larger sibling at Spittal Pond, but this nature reserve, once again run by

---

SWIMMING IN WARWICK LONG BAY

When the sea is choppy the red flag flying from Warwick Long Bay warns all swimmers to stay out of the water. However, even when swimming is permitted, the conditions can be scary for non or poor swimmers and small children. The shallow water quickly and suddenly becomes deep, due to the presence of a shelf on the sea bed, and the bay is also prone to rip currents. So please take heed of the red flag and don't swim in Warwick Long Bay alone. Note there is no lifeguard on duty at this beach.

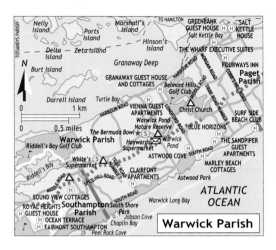

Map labels:
Nelly Island, Ports Island, Marshall's Island, TO HAMILTON, GREENBANK GUEST HOUSE (H) (H) SALT KETTLE HOUSE, Hinson's Island, Salt Kettle Bay, THE WHARF EXECUTIVE SUITES, Delta — Zeta Island, Granaway Deep, FOURWAYS INN, Burt Island, GRANAWAY GUEST HOUSE AND COTTAGES, Belmont Hills Golf Club, Paget Parish, Darrell Island, Turtle Bay, VIENNA GUEST APARTMENTS, Christ Church, SURF SIDE BEACH CLUB, The Bermuda Bowl, Warwick Pond Nature Reserve, BLUE HORIZONS, Warwick Parish, Riddell's Bay Golf Club, Haywards Supermarket, Warwick Pond, ASTWOOD COVE, THE SANDPIPER GUEST APARTMENTS, White's Supermarket, MARLEY BEACH COTTAGES, CLAIRFONT APARTMENTS, Astwood Park, ATLANTIC OCEAN, SOUND VIEW COTTAGES, ROYAL HEIGHTS GUEST HOUSE, Southampton Parish, South Shore Park, Warwick Long Bay, Jobson Cove, OCEAN TERRACE, FAIRMONT SOUTHAMPTON, Chaplin Bay, Peel Rock Cove, **Warwick Parish**
N, 0 — 1 km, 0 — 0.5 miles

ROAD ETIQUETTE

Bermudians drive on the left side of the road. The islands also have a number of roundabouts where you must yield to traffic on the right. Visitors cannot hire cars, but are allowed to rent mopeds and scooters. Anyone riding a moped or scooter must wear a helmet. The official speed limit in Bermuda is 35kph (22mph), although many locals drive at 50kph (31mph)

the Bermuda National Trust, is worth popping into. A well-marked trail guides you along, with information boards to illuminate the flora and fauna encountered en route. Anyone particularly sensitive to poison ivy should watch where they are walking as it creeps around everywhere. The path leads around the south bank of the pond, with the whole reserve spreading across a 4ha (9-acre) site. Look out for the bountiful bird life, which includes wood warblers, herons, sandpipers, grebes and ducks. Sadly, Flo, the legendary flamingo who staged a number of daring escapes from Bermuda Zoo in Hamilton Parish to take up residence in her favourite pond, no longer calls this tranquil setting home.

Astwood Park ★★

This wonderful little coastal park on the south shore is very popular with locals who come here to picnic and also sometimes to get married! Follow the cliffs down to the sheltered, sandy coves, but watch where you stand as there are a few steep drops. Just offshore you can see shadows of the reefs that make for easily accessible snorkelling. Out of the water Astwood is also home to abundant bird life, with different species putting in appearances depending on the season.

Below: Learn more about Bermuda's fauna and flora on the well-marked nature trail at Warwick Pond Nature Reserve.

Warwick Parish at a Glance

BEST TIMES TO VISIT

The sandy South Shore beaches that line Warwick Parish are at their busiest during sweltering July and August days. From April to October it is possible to hire snorkelling gear and other water-sports equipment at the beach club on Horseshoe Bay and from some hotels. Have the beach to yourself on sunny November and December days, when the sea is still warm enough for a dip for many visitors.

GETTING THERE

Bus route 7, which runs from the City of Hamilton to the Royal Naval Dockyard, runs along Warwick's south shore, with bus number 8 cutting through the parish along Middle Road. The pink ferry route from the islands' capital serves Darrell's Wharf and the Belmont Wharf.

GETTING AROUND

Warwick's busy roads mean that it is not advisable to walk along these. Riding a moped/scooter or travelling by bicycle will give you the freedom to fully explore the parish, as will booking a taxi tour. Bus route 7 stops close to Astwood Park and Warwick Long Bay. Those heading for Christchurch and Warwick Pond Nature Reserve should catch the number 8 bus.

WHERE TO STAY

LUXURY

Surf Side Beach Club, 90 South Road, tel: 236-7100, fax: 236-9765, www.surfside bermuda.com This pleasant resort comprises 38 white-washed rooms, apartments and cottages in an attractive cliffside location. Suites have kitchens equipped with refrigerators and cooking facilities. Guests also benefit from a restaurant, bar, an outdoor swimming pool, spa and private beach.

BUDGET

Marley Beach Cottages, South Road, tel: 236-1143, fax: 236-1984. Cottages and studio apartments with dramatic ocean views; all units have a kitchen and private terrace. There is also a freshwater pool, jacuzzi and private beach.

Granaway Guesthouse and Cottage, Harbour Road, tel: 236-3747, fax: 236-3749, www.granaway.com This 18th-century manor house is full of character and retains period features like cedar wood beams. Accommodation is provided on a pleasantly small scale with just five bedrooms being located in the main house. You can also opt to stay in the Granaway Cottage, which was originally where the slaves slept. An immaculately landscaped garden,

outdoor swimming pool, sea views and the pastel-hued rooms all combine to create a relaxing retreat.

The Sandpiper Guest Apartments, 10 South Road, tel: 236-7093, fax: 236-3898, www.bermuda.com/sand piper These clean and modern apartments, which accommodate up to four people, are furnished to a high standard, with private balconies, full kitchens and a separate dining space. There is also an outdoor pool and BBQ area.

Clairfont Apartments, 6 Warwickshire Road, tel: 238-3577, fax: 238-3503, www.clairfontapartments. com Accommodation comes in the form of eight studio rooms or apartments with separate sitting rooms. All units have a fully equipped kitchen and either a private balcony or patio area. The apartments are also situated within easy walking distance of some of Warwick's most attractive beaches.

Vienna Guest Apartments, 63 Cedar Hill, tel: 236-3300, fax: 236-6100, www.bermuda1. com/Vienna The six simply furnished units sleep up to four people and offer views of the Great Sound, Gibb's Hill Lighthouse and Forest Hills. Each apartment has a fully equipped kitchen and a small patio. There is also a communal swimming pool.

Blue Horizons, 93 South Road, tel: 236-6350, fax: 236-9151. Simply furnished units and apartments. Good rates year-round.

LUXURY
Palms Restaurant (*see* Surfside Beach Club). First-class fusion cuisine, crispy spring rolls, Bermudian dishes and freshly grilled meat and fish are all served up in an intimate dining space. During warm summer evenings the sound of the sea caressing the beach lures diners outside to watch the sunset from beneath the towering palms on the raised poolside terrace.

Riddell's Bay Golf & Country Club, 26 Riddell's Bay Road, tel: 238-1060, www.riddells bay.com Light appetizers like lobster ravioli in a Pernod and chive sauce, fresh soups, adventurous salads and fish and grilled meat entrées followed by irresistible desserts feature on the golf club's evening menu, with the cost of your meal relating to the number of courses ordered (two–five). The local pan-seared mahi mahi fish cooked with black rum and banana chutney

comes highly recommended, as does the lime cheesecake.

MID-RANGE
Paw Paws, 87 South Road, tel: 236-7459. Cooks at this popular local restaurant conjure up a variety of North American, Caribbean and European-influenced dishes alongside Bermudian favourites like codfish cakes. One of the key ingredients in the menu is the paw paw (papaya) and this fruit also takes pride of place in the interior murals.

BUDGET
Four Star Pizza, 55 Middle Road, tel: 232-0123. Pizza, chicken wings and a few Chinese dishes are available from the Warwick branch of this takeaway restaurant chain. They also operate a delivery service.

Brenda's Poolside Diner & Ice Cream Parlour, 93 South Road. Snack bar serving burgers, other fast-food snacks and ice cream.

Hayward's Supermarket, 49 Middle Road, tel: 232-3395. This centrally located food store is handy for self-caterers.

White's Supermarket, 22 Middle Road, tel: 238-1050. Supermarket and pharmacy.

Lindo's Family Foods, 128 Middle Road, tel: 236-1344. Another handy food store.

Spicelands Riding Centre, PO Box 1980, tel: 238-8212, fax: 295-4946, www.spicelands riding.com Join one of the early morning or afternoon horseback trail rides along the islands' beautiful south shore. The centre also offers private horse-riding lessons.

Belmont Hills Golf Club, 97 Middle Road, tel: 236-6400, fax: 236-0694, www.belmont hills.com Billing itself as a semi-private golf club, Belmont Hills offers day membership to its 18-hole course. You can also hire clubs, take lessons or purchase any forgotten essentials in the pro-shop. At present dining is a relaxed affair in the club's café, but a new restaurant is being constructed.

Riddell's Bay Golf & Country Club, 26 Riddell's Bay Road, tel: 238-1060, www.riddells bay.com This private 18-hole golf course welcomes visitors.

Snorkel Equipment Rental, Warwick Long Bay Beach, tel: 799-5657.
Scooter/moped Rental see Paget (page 95) and Southampton (page 109) listings.

10
Southampton Parish

Hilly Southampton Parish in the west of Bermuda is a leisure oasis that boasts a string of beaches including perhaps the most famous of them all, **Horseshoe Bay** on its South Shore. In **Church Bay Park** and **West Whale Bay Park** there are stretches of coastline that have been preserved for the public to enjoy free of charge.

Southampton is also something of a Mecca for golfers as there are two golf courses, the **Fairmont Southampton Golf Club** and the **Port Royal Golf Club**, as well as a driving range at the **Bermuda Golf Academy**. History buffs won't find historic houses or museums in Southampton, but there are the remains of a fort and a well-preserved gun battery on the parish's South Shore, as well as **Gibb's Hill Lighthouse**, one of the oldest iron lighthouses in the world, which offers perhaps the finest views of Bermuda.

Horseshoe Bay ***

This gorgeous pink sand beach has been voted one of the world's top 10 beaches with good reason. The wide sands sweep around in a horseshoe shape, with a rocky outcrop at the western end offering a good spot to take in its entirety. The facilities are good, with lifeguards on duty in the summer months and the **Horseshoe Bay Beach House** on hand with some fast food, showers and changing rooms. **Horseshoe Bay Beach Rentals**, meanwhile, offer snorkel gear, body boards and sun umbrellas.

ATLANTIC OCEAN · ST GEORGE · St George's · Hamilton · Sandys · Pembroke · HAMILTON · Smith's · Devonshire · Paget · Warwick · Southampton

---

DON'T MISS

*** Horseshoe Bay: this sweeping horseshoe-shaped bay is widely regarded as Bermuda's best beach.
*** Southampton's Golf Courses: play a leisurely round of golf as you admire those Atlantic views.
** Gibb's Hill Lighthouse: come here for the unforgettable views and cosy café.
** Southampton's Coastal Parks: escape the crowds on the beach.

Opposite: *The world's tallest cast-iron lighthouse, Gibb's Hill Lighthouse, stands 36m (117ft) high.*

From Horseshoe Bay Beach you can head east and hook up with the South Shore Park that will take you up towards Warwick Long Bay, and buses on to the rest of Bermuda. Alternatively you can catch the funky old bus that snakes up to the landmark Fairmont Southampton hotel, where a variety of lunch and dinner options await.

Above: *At the top of the list of Bermuda's best beaches – Horseshoe Bay.*

Gibb's Hill Lighthouse ★★

The world's tallest cast-iron lighthouse on Gibb's Hill has vaulted 36m (117ft) into the heavens since 1846. What makes it even more remarkable is that it travelled the length of the Atlantic to get here, having been shipped over in parts from the UK. It is still very much an operational lighthouse and it is said that sailors can pick up its powerful beam from as far as 65km (40 miles) away. Local legend has it that some Southampton citizens put away their oil lamps when it first started operating, thinking it would illuminate their homes.

Even for those with no head for heights the views from the base are stunning as you can see large swathes of Bermuda on all sides below. You are taking in the views in good company – Queen Elizabeth II stood here in 1953 and was said to have been very taken with what she saw, giving it the new name of Queen's View, which is now marked on a plaque.

Those willing to defy vertigo can hike up the 185 steps for the impressive views of Bermuda and the surrounding ocean and reefs; watch out also for various lighthouse paraphernalia as you go. Afterwards you can indulge in tea and cakes or a filling breakfast in the wonderfully old-world tearoom that nestles at the foot of the lighthouse. The 21st century seems a long

BEST BEACHES

Horseshoe Bay,
Southampton Parish.
Elbow Beach,
Paget Parish.
Tobacco Bay,
St George's Parish.
John Smith's Beach,
Smith's Parish.
Warwick Long Bay,
Warwick Parish.

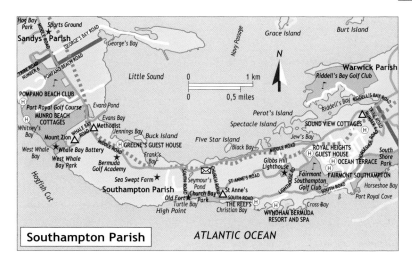

Southampton Parish   ATLANTIC OCEAN

way away as you idle over egg and muffins up here, and life seems to move at a slower pace. Open daily 09:00–16:30, tel: 238-8069.

Southampton's Coastal Parks ★★

New steps have recently been built right down into the beautiful little cove at **Church Bay Park**, offering even easier access to this charming waterfront spot. Avoid the temptation to follow everyone else straight down to the ocean if you are interested in Bermuda's bountiful military history. It may not be the best preserved site on the islands, but on a small rise above the sands you can stand where a fort once stood in the 17th century.

The steep cliffs soon reveal an unspoilt patch of coral pink sand, and turquoise waters that are dotted with the dark shadows of rocks and reef. Church Bay is Southampton's finest snorkelling spot and you can step straight off the rocks or beach and immediately be swimming amongst brightly coloured parrotfish and myriad other marine life. In summer you can rent snorkel gear as well as other beach equipment in the park. The further you swim, the better the experience becomes as you enter the world of the reef proper.

ROAD RASH

Taking a moped around the islands is one of the most fun things you can do on Bermuda and it is a great way to get around, but it is also one of the most dangerous. Most locals you chat to will have experienced 'road rash' at some point and all too many visitors end up with a painful skin scrape too.

BERMUDIAN CUISINE

Bermudian cuisine is influenced by culinary traditions from around the globe, with the quintessential English afternoon tea and the spicy fish chowder (see page 23) both originating from Great Britain. West African influences are displayed in the Bermudian love of bananas, with banana scallops and banana fritters featuring on many a dessert menu. Bananas are even served as an accompaniment to the traditional Sunday breakfast of salted codfish.

Heading further west the along the south shore of Southampton brings you to **West Whale Bay Park**. The military installation here is far more impressive than the one at Church Bay. Just head up the hill to the west of the car park and you emerge at the remains of sturdy coastal defences, the **Whale Bay Battery**, which operated from the 19th century through to the end of World War II. There are no big guns, but you can see where they stood peering out over the ocean, guarding over the improbably named Hog Fish Cut and the threat posed to the Royal Naval Dockyard in Sandys, and you can walk in the footsteps of the soldiers who garrisoned the battery. Look out also for evidence of an older fort that curls just outside the front of the battery.

A more recent addition is the **Port Royal Golf Course**, which runs west of here; you can watch the players hack their way around the fairways and even see some action on the putting greens. This is one of the most appealing courses on the islands and shares the same sweeping ocean views as the fort. Back down the hill to the east, West Whale Beach also has a couple of picnic benches where you can relax, take in the views and watch herons hunting for lizards in the undergrowth.

Boat Bay *

The cresent-shaped private beach at the Wyndham Hotel, with its narrow strip of pale sand, is nothing extraordinary in itself; however, the bay itself has an intriguing history. Originally named Hunt's Bay, these waters are the site of a 17th-century shipwreck, which was grounded offshore in 1661. Many of those on board drowned. Eighty years later the hapless ship fell victim

Left: *Lap up the dramatic sea views as you play a round at one of Bermuda's public courses – the Port Royal Golf Course in Southampton.*
Opposite: *An old gun emplacement at Whale Bay Battery overlooks the Port Royal Golf Course.*

to a Spanish privateer, Francisco Lopez, who raided the wreck and skipped off with his booty before the Bermudian authorities, in two sloops, were able to stop him.

Southampton's Golf Courses ***

Keen golfers will be in heaven in Southampton Parish. The aforementioned **Port Royal Golf Course** is one of the cheaper options on Bermuda and it can sometimes be easier getting a tee-off time here than at the more exclusive courses. That said, it is a beautiful par 71 course designed by legendary golf guru Robert Trent Jones, boasting trim fairways bounded by subtropical vegetation and fairly forgiving bunkers.

Nearby, the **Fairmont Southampton Golf Club**, which tumbles around the hillside beneath the hulking hotel, also welcomes visiting golfers, though it is easier to secure a round if you are a guest at the hotel or (as with most of Bermuda's courses) book through the concierge at your hotel. Curiously, the 18-hole golf course is a par 54. While it may not test experienced golfers looking for a challenge it is fun to play nonetheless. If you are just looking to brush up on your swing in practice before tackling the islands' tough courses, you can whack balls at the Bermuda Golf Academy to your heart's content.

BERMUDIAN TIME

Some exasperated expats have coined the term 'Bermudian time' to describe the frustration caused by many Bermudians being late for every meeting. It seems being slightly tardy is more than socially acceptable, but perish the visitor who tries to pull the same outrageous trick on a deeply offended local.

Southampton Parish at a Glance

Most people visit Southampton to relax and unwind on the parish's beaches or play at the Port Royal and Fairmont Southampton golf courses. Golf can be played at any time of year, although the humidity can be uncomfortably high between Jun and Aug. Southampton's beaches (public and private) are in full swing between mid-May and mid-Oct. If you want to relax on a secluded stretch of sand and don't mind the slightly cooler sea temperatures then Nov and Dec are ideal months to visit.

Bus numbers 7 and 8, which run between the City of Hamilton and the Royal Naval Dockyard, serve Southampton. To reach Southampton from St George's or the airport you will need to catch bus number 3, 10 or 11 and then change in the City of Hamilton. The Rockaway Express (green route) is a high-speed ferry link between the parish and the capital. Guests at the Fairmont Southampton Princess can travel by private boat from the Fairmont Hamilton Princess in the capital (see page 40).

The majority of Southampton's south shore attractions are located close to bus stops on bus route number 7. If you alight near the Henry VIII Pub and Restaurant, Gibb's Hill

Lighthouse is a short uphill walk. Bus number 8 runs along Middle Road, which overlooks the parish's north nhore. It stops near the Port Royal Golf Course, with West Whale Bay just a short walk away from here.

LUXURY

Fairmont Southampton Princess, 101 South Road, tel: 238-8000, fax: 238-8968, www.fairmont.com Bermuda's largest resort hotel will keep even the most demanding family happy, with a golf course, private beach, tennis courts, outdoor pool and what many regard as Bermuda's best spa. Spacious guest rooms have their own balconies, offering great sea views. An innovative range of private dining experiences allows guests to enjoy romantic candlelit dinners on their private balconies or the beach. **The Reefs**, 56 South Road, tel: 238-0222, fax: 238-8372, www.thereefs.com This 65-room cottage colony enjoys a seafront location and has light and stylish rooms. The resort also has an outdoor pool, tennis courts, a small fitness centre and three restaurants. **Pompano Beach Club**, 36 Pompano Beach Road, tel: 234-0222, fax: 234-1694, www.pompano.bm This luxurious ocean-front cottage colony has spacious guest accommodation decorated in

traditional Bermudian style, as well as a heated pool, two whirlpools, tennis courts, fitness centre and a spa that all have Atlantic views. The club also has its own restaurants, bars and a water-sports centre. **Wyndham Bermuda Resort and Spa**, 6 Sonesta Drive, tel: 238-8122, fax: 238-8465, www.wyndham.com The Sonesta Beach Resort, which was battered by hurricane Fabian back in 2003, has been reinvented as the Wyndham, with its classically styled guest rooms, three private beaches, spa, dive shop, water park and water-sports equipment rental.

BUDGET

Munro Beach Cottages, 2 Port Royal Golf Course Road, tel: 234-1175, fax: 234-3528, www.munrobeach.com Modest accommodation with private kitchens. It is worth paying the small premium for an ocean view. **Ocean Terrace**, tel: 238-0019, fax: 238-4673. Self-contained units with fully equipped kitchens and a veranda area. The apartments also have good views and a swimming pool. **Sound View Cottages**, 9 Bowe Lane, tel: 238-0064. Located within easy walking distance of Southampton's best public beaches, this pleasantly low-key place has just three rooms.

Southampton Parish at a Glance

Each apartment has its own kitchenette.

Greene's Guesthouse, 71 Middle Road, tel: 238-0834, fax: 238-8980. This modern guesthouse has just six basic but clean rooms and a swimming pool. For a more luxurious stay consider renting the two-bedroom apartment.

Royal Heights Guesthouse, 4 Crown Hill, tel: 238-0043, fax: 238-8445. Located towards the top of Lighthouse hill this friendly guesthouse is convenient for Gibb's Hill Lighthouse and is a good budget option. Guest rooms are comfortable, but on the small side.

WHERE TO EAT

LUXURY

Newport Room (*see* Fairmont Southampton Princess). Widely regarded as one of Bermuda's best restaurants, the Newport Room is all about fine dining and elegant surroundings. The menu is modern French; formal dress and reservations are required.

The Waterlot Inn (*see* Fairmont Southampton Princess). Built in 1670, this historic building reclines in a hard-to-beat waterfront location. The candlelit interior of this traditional inn is a great place for a romantic meal, while dining moves outside in the warmer summer months. Fine quality steaks that have been hung for a minimum of three

weeks, and are broiled at 180°C, are the signature dishes of the restaurant. For a spot of real indulgence opt for the Surf and Turf (an 8oz filet steak and Maine lobster tail) or enjoy a pre-dinner drink and cigar in front of the fire.

The Cedar Room (*see* Pompano Beach Club). Panoramic Atlantic views and a fine-dining menu that features the likes of snails, grilled quail, rockfish and cream cheese soufflé are this restaurant's winning ingredients.

Coconuts (*see* The Reefs). During the season (April to November) Coconuts offers alfresco dining on the beach. A simple lunch menu features sandwiches, baguettes and salads, while the evening menu is more formal with delicate fish dishes being the highlight.

MID-RANGE

Henry VIII Pub and Restaurant, 56 South Road, tel: 238-1977. Located just below Gibb's Hill Lighthouse, this south shore restaurant has been serving an English-style menu in a mock-Tudor building for more than 35 years. Mainstays on the menu include Bermuda fish, shellfish, poultry and English roasts and steak and kidney pie. During the summer season there is nightly entertainment in the pub.

Sazanami (*see* Wyndham Bermuda Resort & Spa). Serves tempura, sashimi and sushi in a relaxed setting.

BUDGET

Gibb's Hill Lighthouse Tearoom, 68 St Anne's Road, tel: 238-8679. This characterful eatery housed in the lighthouse is full of interesting bits and bobs and offers superb views. Combine this with friendly staff and good, affordable food then you can't really go wrong. A great spot for breakfast or a private party.

Traditions, 2 Middle Road, tel: 234-3770. This small restaurant housed in a little green hut serves home-made food to eat in or take away. The cook also conjures up reasonable Chinese cuisine.

USEFUL CONTACTS

Port Royal Golf and Tennis Club, 5 Middle Road, tel: 234-0974. This public course is open to visitors.

Oleander Cycles, 8 Middle Road, tel: 234-0629.

Fairmont Southampton Golf Club, South Road, tel: 239-6952.

Pompano Beach Watersports Centre (*see* Pompano Beach Club).

Fantasea Bermuda, Waterlot Inn, tel: 238-1833.

Bermuda Golf Academy, 10 Industrial Park Road, tel: 238-8800.

Church Bay Snorkelling, Church Bay, tel: 799-5657.

11
Sandys Parish

Somewhat confusingly pronounced 'Sands', this is one of the most captivating of all the parishes in Bermuda. The westernmost parish is an oasis full of attractions, ranging from old forts and parks through to what, in the **Royal Naval Dockyard**, is one of Bermuda's genuine must-see attractions.

Sandys was once the sole preserve of the Royal Navy who heavily fortified Ireland Island and made the Royal Naval Dockyard the 30ha (75-acre) 'Gibraltar of the West', a bulwark against the emerging Americans. The military legacy has been put to good use, with the Dockyard reinvented as a leisure hub, popular with both locals and tourists, and with a string of things to see and do, as well as eating options and direct ferries from Hamilton and St George. Here you can choose whether to leaf through layers of history at the **Maritime Museum**, delve into the past at the **Commissioner's House**, get more active by snorkelling with tropical fish at the **Snorkel Park,** or swim with bottlenose dolphins at **Dolphin Quest**.

The most interesting settlement is Somerset, a pleasantly untouristy slice of Bermuda, which is home to a couple of nature reserves. Green Sandys also boasts the **Hog Bay Park**, the **Gilbert Nature Reserve** and the lush grounds of the **Heydon Trust**, in a parish where there is plenty of opportunity to 'get away from it all'. The main historical attraction outside of the Royal Naval Dockyard is the **Scaur Hill Fort and Park**, which vies with Fort St Catherine when it comes to Bermuda's most

ATLANTIC OCEAN · ST GEORGE · St George's · Hamilton · Sandys · Smith's · Pembroke · Devonshire · HAMILTON · Paget · Warwick · Southampton

---

DON'T MISS

*** Scaur Hill Fort and Park: hilltop fort offering sweeping views of the Great Sound.
*** Bermuda Maritime Museum: delve into Bermuda's maritime museum in deeply historical surrounds.
*** Dolphin Quest: chance to swim with dolphins.
** Hog Bay Park: great snorkelling.
** Somerset Village: tranquil seaside village with two first-rate restaurants.

Opposite: *Sturdy old fortified walls and a drawbridge at the Royal Naval Dockyard.*

Above: *The coastal stretch of Hog Bay Park is a good place for spotting parrotfish.*

impressive fortifications. From here the views, as they so often are in Sandys Parish, are captivating.

Hog Bay Park ★★

It often looks as if there is no arable land in Bermuda, but a 15-minute walk through this 15ha (38-acre) park to the coast at Hog Bay will soon dis-abuse you of this notion. It may not quite be the Great Plains, but there is a patchwork of small plots, many of which have been farmed for centuries. You will also come across old farm buildings and outhouses, and disused equipment like an old lime kiln just to the east of the main path. Look out also for the phalanx of dead cedar trees, not the direct result of man's machinations, but actually victims of the cedar blight in the 1940s.

It is a fairly steep descent down to the ocean and it is an attractive spot with dark volcanic rocks contrasting with the startlingly cobalt blue waters. Those too timid to try snorkelling can look out for parrotfish, which can often be seen circling around and rubbing against the rocks.

Somerset ★★

Getting to the town of Somerset is half the fun as you have to cross what is said to be the smallest draw-bridge in the world (it is only 55cm/22in across). It certainly enjoys bijou proportions, looking as if one would be hard pushed to get a rowing boat through the hand-operated bridge, not to mention the yachts that somehow squeeze through. Somerset Village itself is a pleasant little place to relax, with the coastal Somerset Long Bay Park sporting a sandy beach and a nature trail that is popular with ornithologists who come to

BERMUDIAN CIVIL WAR

During the American Civil War Bermuda largely sup-ported the Confederates by supplying their armies. The local economy boomed, especially around St George, where British ships came in for the South's cotton, which was shipped into Bermuda on blockade-busting fast ships, with arms and other supplies going the other way. Sandys, meanwhile, was the only parish to side with the Union.

check out the migratory birds. The local pub, **The Country Squire**, does excellent value local spiny lobster in season to go with its big-screen sport. When the cricket is on, particularly the bi-annual cup game with St George's that is held here, the focus of the parish is firmly set on Somerset Cricket Club.

Springfield and Gilbert Nature Reserve *

Another Bermuda National Trust property, this is a worthwhile diversion on a sunny day. **Springfield**, a colonial-era manor house, and its outbuildings date from the 1740s and are the focal point of the reserve. Unfortunately it is not normally open to the public as it functions as a community centre. The main reason to visit is to enjoy wandering through the 2ha (5-acre) **Gilbert Nature Reserve**, with its thick vegetation and cedar and palmetto palm woodland, to the rear of the house; there are a web of paths to follow and get lost in. You can work your way through from here to join a section of the Railway Trail that connects to Somerset town in the west and Scaur Hill Fort in the east.

Scaur Hill Fort and Park ***

This impressive polygon-shaped fortification rambles across Somerset Island's highest ground and enjoys sweeping views out over the Great Sound. The 61st Foot Regiment started work on the fort back in the 1860s with the aim of guarding against any American land attack on the Royal Naval Dockyard; ironically two centuries later the American 52nd Coast Artillery manned the base during World War II and gave it the rather hideous nickname of 'Cockroach Gully'.

Today you can clamber around the fort, checking out the sunken gun emplacements

Below: *Scaur Hill Fort, situated at Somerset Island's highest point, offers panoramic views over the Great Sound.*

Above: *The tiny white-washed Heydon Trust Chapel dates from the 17th century.*

that once housed the 'disappearing' guns that were designed to protect their gunners from return fire, and then descend to check out the rest of the complex, which covers much of the hill. Still visible is the caponier – a protected passageway that allowed the fort's defenders to dispense small-arms fire in relative safety – which was built with the aim of mowing down advancing enemy troops gathering below.

The main attraction for many visitors is the view, which sweeps spectacularly around stretching from the Royal Naval Dockyard in the west right around to St George's Parish in the extreme east. Take a seat on one of the benches or peer through the viewfinder that is mounted in front of the gun emplacements and enjoy the panorama.

Heydon Trust ★★

At the heart of this pretty 17ha (43-acre) private reserve is a sweet, small whitewashed chapel. It was a tiny dwelling (look out for the miniscule oven behind the altar), built as early as the 17th century, but the multi-denominational Heydon Trust managed to squeeze in and open it as a chapel. Today you are welcome to join in the regular services, including the Gregorian nights, when the haunting chants echo out into the unspoilt subtropical gardens and across the ocean.

The gardens are open from dawn until dusk so you can join the bright red cardinal butterflies and the striking yellow kiskadees exploring the pathways and even link up with a section of the Railway Trail, which will take you further afield to Somerset Town or Somerset Bridge.

Below: *One of the two huge towers at the Clocktower Building, home to the eponymous shopping mall.*

ROYAL NAVAL DOCKYARD

The tragic history of the Dockyard is there for all to see if you travel to it by road. On Ireland Island North a sprawling graveyard rambles away from the road, where the remains of hundreds of labourers lie, whose efforts

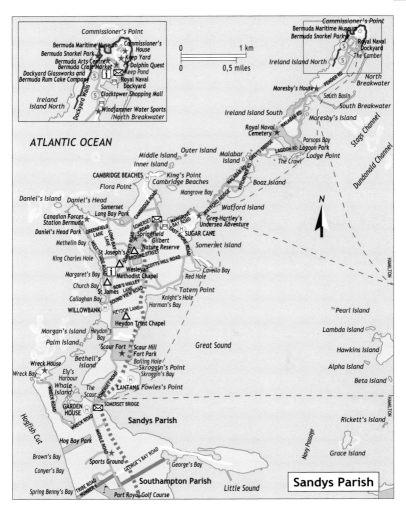

Sandys Parish

to build the Dockyard turned out to be their last. Today the Royal Naval Dockyard is packed with visitor attractions and its darker days are placed firmly in the past. In summer a cute little **tourist road train** rattles around the complex, offering an easy way to get a feel for it all. While you choose where to go also take time to admire

Above: *Ornate glass fish and a plate on sale at the Dockyard Glassworks.*

the grand buildings themselves. The **Clocktower Building** ushers in new arrivals with the voluminous 30m (100ft) twin towers that can be spotted from much of Bermuda: one shows the time and the other the once crucial time of high tide, which was essential for navigating the treacherous local waters. Within the building itself, now called the Clocktower Shopping Mall, you will find the old administration buildings that have been replaced by a phalanx of shops and cafés, very much geared towards tourists.

Housed in the myriad buildings nearby you will also find the award-winning **Bermuda Arts Centre**, which was opened in 1984 and now houses the work of local artists; if you are lucky a few of them will be on hand to discuss their work as you wander amongst workshops where the fragrance of cedar sifts through the air.

Then there is the **Bermuda Craft Market**, in the old Cooperage building, where traditional Bermudian skills, such as quilting, jewellery and cedar work, are kept alive. The former Cooperage is also home to a pub/restaurant for those exhausted after shopping.

Two of the most famous occupants of the Dockyard today are the **Dockyard Glassworks** and **Bermuda Rum Cake Company**. You can watch glass-blowing demonstrations at the glass studio or, under the same roof, sample the legendary rum cakes. The cakes are all infused with rum, but as well as the traditional recipe you can also sample chocolate and banana varieties.

Bermuda Maritime Museum ★★★

Housed within the 2ha (6-acre) fort is this fascinating insight into Bermuda's maritime heritage. Cross the moat that leads through the 9m (30ft) high ramparts and you enter a world of old ships and tall tales, spread across a number of buildings. The main section of the keep is stuffed full of exhibits such as old boats, paintings, photos and gold and silver treasures.

The **Boat Loft** is home to an array of old boats rather than scale models, with nautical flags hanging from the ceiling, which further accentuate the maritime atmosphere. Look out for the old dinghies that used to compete to speed through the reefs and bring passengers and cargo ashore from much larger boats in times gone by. There is also the original Great Storehouse clock and exhibits on fishing and turtle hunting.

The highlight for many is the 'hurricane-proof' **Commissioner's House**, where once the man who ran the Dockyard enjoyed a prime position, raised on a knoll above the keep courtyard. The Commissioner's House was built in 1823, the first building on the islands to use a prefabricated cast and a wrought-iron framework to go with its Welsh slate roof. The wonderful old verandas offer great views of the Dockyard complex and further afield out over Bermuda and the Atlantic; try the nearby ramparts, too, for similarly impressive views.

Inside the building you will find old paintings and charts, as well as exhibits touching on Bermuda's slave history and its connections with Portugal and the West Indies. There is also an exhibit on Bermuda's tourist industry, while the collection of maps on the second floor spans from the 16th to the 19th century. Open daily 09:00–16:30, tel: 234-1418, www.bmm.bm

Dolphin Quest ★★★

If you have ever harboured dreams of meeting 'Flipper' and spending time in the water with

BERMUDIAN SOUVENIRS

Souvenir shops crammed with colourful T-shirts sporting Bermuda logos are located mainly in the City of Hamilton and St George. For a more authentically Bermudian souvenir, seek out items carved from cedar wood, coins transformed into jewellery, Bermuda honey, dolls made from banana leaves, Bermuda rum, Bermuda rum cakes, or even a pair of Bermuda shorts. The Dockyard Glass Company also produces tiny skink figurines.

Below: *Sign advertising the Bermuda Rum Cake Company and Dockyard Glassworks, just two of the shopping outlets at the Royal Naval Dockyard.*

SEA VENTURE

After decades of speculation the wreck of the legendary *Sea Venture* was finally discovered in the 1950s. The ship that brought Sir George Somers and the first settlers to Bermuda today lies off the coast of St George's Parish on the appositely named Sea Venture Flat, having lain there since it was shipwrecked four centuries ago.

these magical mammals then this is the place. Interacting with them elsewhere in Bermudian waters is strictly off limits. Bermuda's Dolphin Quest first opened in 1996 at the Fairmont Southampton Princess Hotel, becoming the third site owned and managed by the marine veterinarians Dr Jay Sweeny and Dr Rae Stone. Just three years after its opening the original dolphin habitat was destroyed by the high waves created by Hurricane Gert as it blew past the islands, and it was relocated to the Maritime Museum. Unlike at some dubious operations around the world, the dolphins here seem to be well cared for, living longer than they would in the wild, with fresh sea water circulating through a sluice and some of the bottlenose dolphins on show today actually born in captivity.

You can choose whether you want to just come and watch the dolphins interact or, for those aged five or over, actually be part of the 'show'. The latter is far more expensive, but deeply rewarding as you get to interact with the dolphins in the water and even gently touch them under supervision from the trainers, a special experience especially with some of the younger dolphins who are learning the ropes and seem to be having as much fun as the human interlopers. You really get to appreciate the speed, size and power of these 273kg (600lb) mammals as they shoot underneath you and shower you with water, before zooming off across the pool.

Below: *Visitors enjoying the hands-on swimming with dolphins experience at Bermuda's Dolphin Quest.*

Note that you cannot take cameras in if you are swimming, though you can buy photos afterwards of your experience, amongst a whole host of dolphin-related paraphernalia in the attached gift shop. Dolphin swimming reservations are essential. Tel: 234-4464, www.dolphinquest.org

Dockyard Water Sports ★★★

If you are unsure of taking your little ones, or yourself for that matter, out into the open ocean for a spot of snorkelling or scuba diving then pop into the Bermuda Snorkel Park (tel: 234-6889). Here you can swim among myriad tropical fish in the lagoon by the keep and even explore the rusting cannons that were hurled in here when they were no longer needed. Nearby, Windjammer Watersports (tel: 234-0250) offer a more adrenaline-filled experience. In season you can hire small sailing boats, kayaks and wind surfboards.

Convict Cemetery ★

The majority of visitors to Sandys' Ireland Island visit the 13 modest graves that sit in the small and peaceful convict cemetery, which is tucked discreetly behind a row of houses. The graveyard, which is managed by the Bermuda National Trust, is, however, all the more poignant when you consider that of the 9000 convicts transported to Bermuda, 2000 died. The uniformly grey stone headstones reveal another tragedy: the identity of just four of those buried in the 13 marked graves is actually known. Those convicts that survived worked as labourers for the British navy and army.

Above: *Locals enjoying a cruise around calm Bermuda waters; it's the best way to really get a feel for the geography of the islands.*

Sandys Parish at a Glance

BEST TIMES TO VISIT

From April to October Sandys Parish takes on a more frenetic edge as the passengers from the large cruise ships spill out into the Royal Naval Dockyard. The sea is also at its warmest in high season, with a range of companies offering water-based activities from helmet diving and snorkelling to jet-skiing. In the winter Sandys adopts a different charm, with tranquil beaches and coves; this is also a pleasant time to don a wetsuit and take part in one of the Dolphin Quest activities, with fewer partici-pants allowing you a more rewarding time with the dolphins. Between November and March there are a number of free tourist activities in the parish including bicycle rides (Tuesdays), guided walks (Thursdays) and various events at the Royal Naval Dockyard (Tuesdays to Thursdays, as well as Saturdays and Sundays).

GETTING THERE

Sandys is at the western end of bus routes number 7 and 8 which run between the City of Hamilton and the Royal Naval Dockyard. Two year-round ferry routes also connect the parish to Hamilton, with the green route stopping at Somerset Bridge and the blue route serving Cavello Bay, Watford Bridge and the Royal Naval Dockyard. From May to

November the orange ferry route links the Royal Naval Dockyard to St George and Hamilton. Taxis from Hamilton to Sandys are surprisingly affordable given the relatively long distance, and the parish can also be reached by moped.

GETTING AROUND

The roads in Sandys are comparatively quiet and it is possible to walk from Somerset to the Royal Naval Dockyard, via Somerset Long Bay Park, although there is not always a footpath and this will take around 45–60 minutes. Bus number 7 also covers this route, with regular services making this a quick and affordable way to travel. Scooter and moped hire is also available at the Royal Naval Dockyard. This flat parish is also a great place for a leisurely cycle.

WHERE TO STAY

LUXURY
Cambridge Beaches, 30 Kings Point Road, tel: 234-0331, fax: 234-3352, www.cam bridgebeaches.com This deluxe cottage colony offers the best of everything, from individually styled guest accommodation with spectacular sea views to suites with infinity pools. Residents also have access to a spa, indoor and outdoor pools, tennis courts, croquet and a putting green, private

beaches, various water sports and a variety of dining options. The five-course dinner served in Tamarisk offers some of the best food on the islands and more than justifies the addi-tional payment for the meal plan. The hotel can organize virtually anything that you want to do in Bermuda, not that many guests actually want to leave the sublime grounds.

MID-RANGE
Willowbank Hotel and Resort, 126 Somerset Road, tel: 234-1616, fax: 234-3373, www.willowbank.bm This cottage colony is actually a non-denominational Christian hotel with light, spacious and well-appointed rooms.

BUDGET
Garden House, 4 Middle Road, tel: 234-1435, fax: 234-3006. This lovely old Bermudian house dates from the 19th century and has accommodation in three cottages. There are no sea views, but the garden does stretch down to Ely Harbour. Guests can also use the saltwater pool and each cottage has its own washer/dryer.

WHERE TO EAT

LUXURY
Tamarisk (*see* Cambridge Beaches). The Scottish chef brings five-course fine dining

to the parish each night, with the most coveted tables located on the outdoor terrace with its stunning bay views. Choose from the likes of beef carpaccio, home-made pâté, fresh Bermudian fish and tender beef and lamb dishes. Reservations are essential.

MID-RANGE

Sea Breeze (see Cambridge Beaches). Between May and October enjoy a more casual dining experience as you look over Long Beach and the Atlantic.

Salt Rock Grill, 27 Mangrove Bay, tel: 234-4502. A menu dominated by seafood and steaks features the likes of grouper chowder, tuna sashimi, lobster and steaks that have been hung for at least four weeks.

BUDGET

Somerset Country Squire, 10 Mangrove Bay, tel: 234-0105. This friendly local pub-restaurant boasts a large terrace overlooking the bay. When the sun isn't shining, or there are big sporting events on, the action moves inside to the basement bar decked out in sporting paraphernalia. The food is good whatever you choose, but the real reason to come here is to feast on Bermuda spiny lobster. During the lobster season there is often a Saturday night promotion where you can buy

a whole or half lobster at a fraction of the price in most of Bermuda's other restaurants.

Beethoven's, Royal Naval Dockyard, tel: 234-5009. Housed in the Clocktower Shopping Mall, this unpretentious café is a good place to grab breakfast, a light lunch or a more substantial meal at weekends.

The Frog & Onion Pub and Restaurant, Royal Naval Dockyard, tel: 234-2900. This English-themed pub serves decent pub food and is housed in the Old Cooperage.

Pirate's Landing, Royal Naval Dockyard, tel: 234-5151. A friendly bar-restaurant serving hearty food.

SHOPPING

The Royal Naval Dockyard with its Clocktower Shopping Mall, Glass-blowing Studio, Pottery, Craft Market and outlet for the Bermuda Rum Cake Company is the place to go shopping in Sandys. Unashamedly geared towards tourists, this is a good place to pick up typically Bermudian souvenirs (see page 116).

TOURS AND EXCURSIONS

EZ Rider, Main Road, Somerset Village, tel: 777-3599. Electric pedal assisted bicycles take the strain out of this two-and-a-half-hour tour.

Enjoy a leisurely two-hour cycle from the Royal Naval Dockyard, through Somerset Village to the Great Sound and Fort Scaur before taking the ferry back to the Dockyard from Cavello Bay.

Hartley's Reef Safari, Watford Bridge Ferry Dock, tel: 234-3535, www.hartleybermuda. com Twice-daily boat tours take passengers to a shallow reef where they then walk along the sea bed wearing an oxygenated helmet. You don't need to have any diving experience to take part.

Bermuda Bell Diving, tel: 535-8707, www.helmetdive. com This three-hour tour departs from the Royal Naval Dockyard and incorporates a 25–30-minute helmet dive.

Jet Ski Speed Adventure, Robinson's Marina, Somerset Bridge, tel: 234-3145. Offering 75-minute guided Jet Ski trips to those over the age of 16. Places are limited to six people per adventure so advance booking is recommended.

USEFUL CONTACTS

Visitor Service Bureau, Royal Naval Dockyard, tel: 234-3824.
Oleander Cycles, King's Wharf, Royal Naval Dockyard, tel: 234-2764.
Bermuda Water Ski Centre, Robinson's Marina, Somerset Bridge, tel: 234-3354.

Travel Tips

Tourist Information

Bermuda Department of Tourism, Global House, 43 Church Street, Hamilton HM 12, Bermuda, tel: 229-0023.
Main Overseas Offices:
UK, Bermuda Department of Tourism, tel: 020 7864 9924.
USA, 675 Fifth Avenue, 20th Floor, New York 10017, tel: 1 800 223 6106;
245 Peachtree Centre Avenue NE, Suite 803, Atlanta, GA 30303, tel: 404 524 1541; and 184 High Street, 4th Floor, Boston, MA 02110-3001, tel: 617 524 1541.
Canada, 1200 Bay Street, Suite 1004, Toronto, Ontario M5R 2A5, tel: 416 923 9600.

Entry Requirements

Anyone entering Bermuda must be in possession of a valid passport. Non-residents must also have a return or onward ticket. Nationals of the UK, USA, Canada and Western Europe do not need any further documentation. For more information about visa requirements, contact any British Embassy, High Commission or Consulate overseas.

Customs

Passengers disembarking in Bermuda must complete a customs declaration (one per family group). The duty-free allowance is limited to 50 cigars, 200 cigarettes, 500g of tobacco, 1 litre of spirits, 1 litre of wine and gifts to the value of $30. Duty is payable on all other items, apart from personal clothing, sports and camera equipment, at a rate of 22.25%.

Health Requirements

You do not need any inoculations to visit Bermuda.

Getting There

By Air: Bermuda is served by direct flights from the UK, USA and Canada. Those travelling from other countries will need to book a connection: British Airways (www.britishairways.com), American Airlines (www.aa.com), Continental Airlines (www.continental.com), Delta Airlines (www.deltaairlines.com), US Airways (www.usairways.com), USA 3000 (www.usa3000.com) and Air Canada (www.aircanada.com).

Airport Transfers: Bermuda's hotels are not allowed to offer a shuttle service to their guests, and you can only catch a bus if your luggage fits on your knee. Airport limousines (eight-to 12-seat minibuses) will pick up passengers who have pre-booked this service only, so ask your hotel to organize this for you or contact one of these companies in advance: **Flood Transport Services** (tel: 295-3589), **Bee Line Transport Ltd** (tel: 293-0303), or **Bermuda Host Ltd** (tel: 293-1334). Taxis also serve the airport and do not need to be booked ahead.

By Sea: A large variety of cruise liners dock in Bermuda throughout the main tourist season (April to October). Those with weekly services from the USA include **Celebrity Cruises** (www.celebrity.com), **Norwegian Cruise Line America** (www.ncl.com), **Radisson Seven Seas Cruises** (www.rssc.com) and **Royal Caribbean International** (www.royalcaribbean.com).

What to Pack

Clothing: Dress in Bermuda tends to be quite conservative but this doesn't mean you can't pack for the weather. In the warmer months stick to lightweight clothing, which lets the skin breathe. Smart casual wear is required in most restaurants for lunch and dinner, and it is advisable for men to pack a jacket and tie for a more formal meal. From November to March the evenings can be quite cold, so a jacket or sweater is a good idea. A lightweight waterproof jacket is recommended at any time of year.

Other Items: Sunglasses, sun hat, sunscreen and a bathing suit are essential between April and October. It is also a good idea to protect your skin from the sun during the winter months. Other fundamentals include camera equipment and photocopies of any important documents, such as your passport and travel insurance.

Money Matters

Bermuda's official currency is the Bermuda dollar, which is pegged against the US dollar (also legal tender on the islands). The Bermuda dollar is a decimal currency with 100 cents to one dollar.

Currency Exchange: Money can be exchanged in the arrivals hall of Bermuda International Airport, at hotels and in banks.

Personal Cheques: Anyone with a US bank account can pay for purchases over $200 with a personal cheque. The Bermuda Financial Network

(tel: 292-1799) will also cash cheques written in US dollars.

Traveller's Cheques: Traveller's cheques in US dollars are accepted in most establishments.

Credit Cards: All major credit cards including Amex, Mastercard and VISA are widely accepted. These cards can also be used to withdraw money from ATMs and over the counter in many banks.

Tipping: Most hotels and restaurants add a 15% service charge to the bill, and this is always clearly indicated. If service is not included you should add 15%. Taxi drivers should be given the same gratuity. Many hotels and resorts also levy set charges for staff gratuities.

Tax: VAT is not charged on purchases made in Bermuda. Tax may, however, be payable when you return home depending on the country's duty-free limits.

Accommodation

Bermuda has a range of accommodation options, from private rooms and apartments to accommodation in small boutique hotels and large resorts. Fractional-ownership properties (similar to time-shares), cottage colonies and rooms at private clubs can also be found on the island. Facilities and room rates vary greatly, but most are of a generally high standard. It is normally wise to book more affordable accommodation in advance. Immigration officials may want to know where you are staying when you arrive.

Eating Out

Bermuda has a surprising array of cafés and restaurants, with everything from sandwich delis, pizzerias and British-style pubs through to Italian, Thai, sushi and fine dining restaurants. Like everything else on the island food isn't cheap; a quick snack and a non-alcoholic drink costs around $10. A more substantial meal for one person will be in the region of $20–$30 for two courses ($40-plus in fine dining restaurants) excluding drinks. As the island's capital, the City of Hamilton has the biggest choice of dining options. One way to cut down on your costs is to buy picnic food from the local shops.

Useful Phrases

Although English is the official language, knowing some local slang or linguistic pleasantries is handy:
Good Day/Afternoon/ Evening • The essential greeting in any social situation.
Bermewjan • Bermudian.
Ace Boy • Best friend.
Going Tawn • This literally means going to town, by which locals mean the City of Hamilton.
Guvmit • Government.
Blinds • Sunglasses.
Dark 'n' Stormy • National Drink of Black Seal rum and local ginger beer.
Backside • Dodgy area of Hamilton around Court Street away from the centre, best avoided.

Transport

Road: The official speed limit on Bermuda's roads is 35kph (22mph); however, most drivers travel at 50kph (31mph). Bermuda has an extensive network of paved roads, but these are often narrow and winding. In order to minimize traffic congestion tourists are not allowed to hire cars. Many visitors rent motorized scooters and mopeds, which are available at outlets across the island.

Buses: Bermuda has a good bus network, with 11 routes running near to most sights of interest. Services are frequent and fares are reasonable, especially when you purchase multiple tickets, or a transportation pass. Public buses are pink and bus stops are identified by pink or blue poles (there are also stone shelters at many stops). Fares can be paid with cash (exact fare and coins only), tokens, pre-purchased tickets or transportation passes that are valid for one, three, four, or seven consecutive days. A monthly pass giving unlimited access to buses and ferries is also available. Children under five years old travel free of charge, with those under 16 years of age entitled to a reduced fare. Anyone in possession of a valid student identity card can also purchase discounted travel passes. Transfer tickets, valid for 30 minutes, are available from the driver for anyone who needs to change buses in order to complete their journey. Any baggage that you have must fit on your knee otherwise you will not be able to travel, which is frustrating as many of the buses stop at the airport.

Ferries: Sea Express (www.sea express.bm) operate a number of ferries and catamarans, which provide a pleasant way of getting around Bermuda. Routes are colour coded and the green, blue and pink routes operate year-round. The Green Route connects Hamilton and Rockaway (Southampton), the Blue Route runs between Hamilton and the Royal Naval Dockyard, and the Pink Route links Paget to Warwick. From the middle of May through to mid-November there is also an Orange Route service between Hamilton and St George, which travels via the Royal Naval Dockyard. Bus tickets, tokens and transportation passes are all valid for travel by boat.

Taxis: Taxis can be pre-booked by telephone, caught at taxi ranks and outside hotels, or hailed from the street. The fare structure depends on the number of passengers. If you are sharing a taxi with people that you don't know, the driver is allowed to fix the price that each person/couple will pay. Although the flag fall is quite high, when compared to everything else in Bermuda taxis are not as expensive as you might expect. A one–four passenger journey from the airport to Hamilton costing around $25–$30.

Minibuses: Minibuses accommodating 8–12 passengers operate along limited routes, and can only be used by prior arrangement. For more information, call the companies that provide airport transfers (see Getting There, page 122).

Bicycles: It is possible to rent bicycles by the day or by the week. Unless you stick to the Railway Trail and other paths, you will be on the same narrow, hilly and often traffic-choked roads as everyone else, so this is not that good a way of travelling.

Horse-drawn Carriages: Unashamedly geared towards tourists, a horse-drawn carriage (usually found at the cruise ship

CONVERSION CHART		
FROM	**TO**	**MULTIPLY BY**
Millimetres	Inches	0.0394
Centimetres	Inches	0.3937
Metres	Yards	1.0936
Metres	Feet	3.281
Kilometres	Miles	0.6214
Square kilometres	Square miles	0.386
Hectares	Acres	2.471
Litres	Pints	1.760
Kilograms	Pounds	2.205
Tonnes	Tons	0.984
To convert Celsius to Fahrenheit: x 9 ÷ 5 + 32		

terminals or on the City of Hamilton's Front Street during the main summer months) can be a pleasant way to explore St George and the islands' capital.

Business Hours

Office Hours: Mon–Fri, 09:00–17:00.
Post Offices: Mon–Fri, 08:00–17:00.
Banks: Mon–Fri, 09:00–16:30.
Shops: Mon–Sat, 09:00–17:00.
Cafés/restaurants: Mon–Sat, 11:30–14:30 and 18:00–22:00, some also open on Sunday.

Time Difference

Bermuda operates on GMT-4. Daylight saving is in effect from the first Sunday in April to the last Sunday in October.

Communications

Telephones: There are no local area codes in Bermuda. To dial Bermuda from overseas or from a cell phone registered in a different

ROAD SIGNS

Aside from those delineating distances, or directing you to main attractions, road signs are scarce in Bermuda. One useful navigational tool is to look out for the bus stops, as the pink and blue poles will help you determine what direction you are travelling in. Pink indicates that the buses are heading towards the City of Hamilton, and blue shows that they are heading away from it.

country, the local seven-digit number must be prefixed with the international dialling code 1-441.
Post: Airmail post received at the Hamilton General Post Office (GPO) before 09:30 is dispatched on the same day. For estimated delivery times of air and surface mail, ask at the post office.
International Data Express: The GPO also offers an express mail service, with a 48-hour delivery time to most destinations.

Electricity

Bermuda has a 110 volt, 60 AC electricity system. US plugs and adaptors with two-pin flat-pronged plugs will fit into plug sockets; however, Bermuda's plugs actually have a third round pin. Many hotels will be able to provide you with an adaptor.

Weights and Measures

Weights and measures in Bermuda are metric, with distances measured in kilometres, and mass in grams and kilograms.

Health Precautions

Anyone visiting Bermuda should take precautions against overexposure to the sun, such as wearing sunscreen, light clothing and sun hats. Dehydration can also be a problem, making it important to drink plenty of water. There is no fresh water source in Bermuda; the islands' roofs collect rainwater that is stored for later use. The locals drink tap water and it is safe to do

so; however, it is possible to buy purified water and mineral water. An adequate supply of any prescription medication should be packed, as well as re-placement contact lenses or a spare set of spectacles. Precautions should also be taken against sexually transmitted diseases.

Health Services

Hotels and other accommoda-tion establishments will be able to contact a doctor in the case of non-urgent medical care. Pharmacists are also well trained and should be able to help with minor ailments. Bermuda's King Edward VII Memorial Hospital is located in Paget, and the standard of care is reasonable, although those requiring more complex medical treatment are often transferred to hospitals in the USA. Dial 911 to call an ambulance. Medical care in Bermuda is expensive, so it is essential to take out adequate insurance prior to travelling.

Personal Safety

Bermuda is a safe place, with low crime rates and, although there are some drug-related offences, tourists rarely fall vic-tim to serious crime. Carrying valuables securely and out of sight and not walking alone in the dark will keep you safe. Report crime immediately.

Emergencies

In an emergency dial 911 and specify the required service: ambulance, police or fire brigade.

Etiquette

Greetings: Bermudians will generally greet you and enquire about your health before entering into any kind of discussion. Visitors to the island should extend their hosts the same courtesy.

Clothing: Beachwear should be restricted to the swimming pool or beach. It is an offence to ride a moped or scooter with a bare chest.

Language

Bermuda's official language is English, which many Bermudians speak with a unique English-American twang.

Festivals

January–February: **Bermuda Festival of the Performing Arts**. Jazz, classical, dance and drama acts from around the world take part in this six-week program of events, www.bermudafestvial.org

February: **Bermuda Love Festival**.

March/April: **Bermuda Kite Festival** (*see* page 22).

April: **Bermuda International Film Festival**.

October: **Bermuda Music Festival**. National and international jazz and rhythm and blues musicians fill stages in the Royal Naval Dockyard during this extravaganza.

November: **Bermuda Culinary Arts Festival**. Week-long food festival with demonstrations by locally and internationally renowned chefs.

Other Events:
A raft of events takes place in Bermuda throughout the year.

For current information check the Bermuda Department of Tourism website: www.bermudatourism.com

January: **Bermuda International Race Weekend**. Walks and races of varying lengths help locals and visitors stick to their New Year's resolutions.

April: **Bermuda Annual Exhibition**. Formerly the Agricultural Show, this three-day event takes place in the Botanical Gardens and is an exhibition of flowers, fruit, vegetables, cakes, livestock, equestrian skills and crafts.

April: **XL Capital Bermuda Open Tennis Championship**.

April: **Bermuda Open Squash Championship**.

April: **Peppercorn Ceremony** (*see* pages 44–45).

May–July and September–October: **Beating Retreat Ceremonies** (*see* page 21).

May–June: **Various Yacht Races**. A host of yacht races take place in Bermuda's waters, including the International Race Week with competitors from the UK, USA, Canada and Bermuda.

July–October: **Concerts in the Park**. Open-air concerts held on Sunday afternoons, offering everything from jazz and gospel to rock and pop.

August: **Around the Island Race**. Competitors take to the water in powerboats.

September: **CD&P Bermuda Grand Prix**. A four-day cycle race open to amateurs and professional cyclists.

December: **BUEI Christmas Boat Parade**. Elaborately decorated boats take to Hamilton harbour, and there is also a firework display. This is just one of the islands' festive events.

HEALTH HAZARDS

There are no major health risks associated with visiting Bermuda. The biggest risk to your health is the sun, with sunburn, sunstroke and dehydration all common. Stomach upsets caused by a change in diet also arise. Portuguese men-of-war can be a problem in the ocean, though affected beaches usually have signs warning of what to do in the event of an attack. Stinging fish can also be a problem.

GOOD READING

Practical information on Bermuda:
Davidson, Cecile (2003) *Hiking Bermuda*. Vagnet Publishing.
Background on Bermuda:
Ritchie, Harry (1998) *The Last Pink Bits*. Sceptre.
Benchley, Peter (1976) *The Deep*. Hutchinson.
Useful websites:
Bermuda Tourism www.bermudatourism.com
The website www.bermuda-online.org is also a useful resource when planning your trip.

INDEX